THE POWER PLAY JOURNAL

The Power Play Journal

Battle-Tested Strategies & Reflections for Impactful Leadership

E. Tinna Jackson

Published by Game Changer Publishing

Paperback ISBN: 978-1-964811-36-9
Hardcover ISBN: 978-1-964811-37-6
Digital ISBN: 978-1-964811-38-3

www.GameChangerPublishing.com

DEDICATION

To Nina, Lola, Ernest, Jeffrey, and Michael
Your strength and resilience in your battles helped shape who I am today.

READ THIS FIRST

Just to say thanks for buying and reading my book, I would like to give you a complimentary strategy session with me, no strings attached!

Scan the QR Code Here:

The Power Play Journal

Battle-Tested Strategies & Reflections
for Impactful Leadership

E. Tinna Jackson

www.GameChangerPublishing.com

FOREWORD

I have had the honor of working with many talented individuals. Among them, Tinna Jackson stands out not just for her remarkable abilities but also for the incredible journey of growth and leadership she has undertaken. I first met Tinna when she was a rising star, full of potential and driven by a deep commitment to making a difference. From those early days, it was clear that she possessed an innate understanding of what it takes to lead—an understanding that has only deepened with time and experience.

Witnessing Tinna's evolution into the leader she is today has been inspiring. Her journey epitomizes the power of perseverance, continuous learning, and, most importantly, emotional intelligence. In the high-stakes world of politics, where decisions often impact millions, Tinna's ability to navigate complex challenges with grace, insight, and empathy has made her an invaluable asset.

Tinna is a dedicated student of leadership, constantly seeking to refine her skills and broaden her understanding. Her experiences in various high-pressure roles have given her a unique perspective that she shares generously with others. She knows what it means to lead under fire, to make tough decisions, and to do so with a steady hand and a compassionate heart. These are not just qualities that she preaches; they are qualities she embodies in every aspect of her life and work.

This book reflects Tinna's extraordinary journey. It is a culmination of years spent studying, practicing, and mastering the art of leadership. But more than that, it is a guide for leaders at all levels—whether you are a seasoned executive, an emerging leader, or someone striving to make a difference in your community. The insights contained within these pages are not theoretical; they are battle-tested strategies that have been honed in the real world under the most demanding conditions.

As someone who has seen Tinna's growth firsthand, I can say with confidence that the wisdom she imparts in this book can be life-changing. Her approach to leadership is grounded in reality and infused with a deep understanding of the human condition. She knows that at the heart of every great leader is the ability to connect with others, to understand their needs, and to lead them with both strength and empathy. This is the essence of emotional intelligence, and it is what makes Tinna's leadership so powerful.

For those of us who have had the privilege of working with Tinna, her influence has been nothing short of transformative. She has a way of bringing out the best in those around her, of challenging them to reach higher, to do better, and to lead with integrity. This book is a testament to that influence. It is a roadmap for leaders who aspire to achieve success in a way that is meaningful and sustainable.

The challenges we all face are complex and ever-changing. But with leaders like Tinna Jackson, I am confident we have the tools and the talent to meet those challenges head-on. I urge you to read this book not just as a guide but as a companion on your own leadership journey. Let Tinna's insights inspire you, challenge you, and ultimately empower you to become the leader you were meant to be. I know that her wisdom will have a lasting impact on all who read these pages.

— Sharon Fountain
   President, Performance Development Consultants, LLC

TABLE OF CONTENTS

PREFACE

In the grueling environment of 1980s Southeast D.C., a little girl grew up surrounded by the complex dynamics of a large family. As the only girl with four brothers, a Filipino mother, and a black military father, many perceived her as well-protected and cherished. However, beneath this façade lay a reality marred by deep-seated vulnerabilities and silent struggles. This little girl, seemingly quiet and reserved, was grappling with emotions far beyond her years—anger and a relentless drive for self-preservation. Her journey, a testament to the human spirit, is one that many can relate to, evoking a sense of empathy and connection.

I was that girl, and my journey wasn't paved with the usual childhood joys; instead, it was scattered with obstacles that forced me to develop skills that many leaders take years to cultivate. Early on, I learned the art of strategic planning—meticulously creating a safe space within my room where I could lock out the chaos of my environment. Here, in this self-made sanctuary adorned with poster boards of my favorite artists and my own artwork, I not only found escape but an opportunity to build a foundation for my future.

My resilience was forged in the solitude of my crafted space, where I immersed myself in books, educational games, and creative pursuits. Each activity was a deliberate choice, not just for entertainment but for personal development. I was not just passing time but preparing myself for a different life outside my current reality. This approach to self-education was my first foray into strategic development. I learned to see beyond immediate challenges and envision a future filled with possibilities.

As I advanced through school, using educational games to enhance my writing and critical thinking skills, I applied these competencies to secure opportunities that would lead me away from my troubled environment. Writing powerful essays won me admission to schools outside my Southeast neighborhood, one step further away from the tumult of my home life. This strategic relocation wasn't just about physical distance; it was a calculated move to surround myself with peers who matched my ambition and creativity, to expand my support network, and to continue on my path of self-directed leadership development.

My educational journey carried me into prestigious roles within the U.S. Senate and eventually to a national political committee. Here, the leadership skills honed in the quiet moments of my youth became the bedrock of my professional success. I learned to navigate complex power dynamics and bureaucratic landscapes, applying my early lessons in resilience and strategic thinking to influence and lead effectively.

Now a certified executive coach and emotional intelligence practitioner, I consider these formative years the genesis of my leadership journey. My mantra—Elevate, Excel, Empower—echoes the lessons I learned from my strategic self-education. In my leadership development programs, based on the principles of emotional intelligence, I impart these skills to others, helping them navigate their personal and professional challenges.

I wrote this book, *The Power Play Journal: Battle-Tested Strategies & Reflections for Impactful Leadership*, to serve as a comprehensive playbook for leadership across all professional and personal life. It's designed to equip readers with the tools and insights needed to excel in leading themselves and their families, organizations, and businesses. At the heart of this guide is profound advocacy for emotional intelligence—an essential component that profoundly influences leadership style and effectiveness.

With this book, I aim to inspire and educate readers on the transformative power of emotional intelligence, enabling them to navigate complex relationships and scenarios with grace and authority. I also hope to empower readers to cultivate a leadership approach that is not only effective but also deeply empathetic and informed.

HOW TO USE THIS JOURNAL

This journal is designed to catalyze your personal and professional evolution. Each section is crafted to provoke thought and spur action. Begin by engaging with the reflective questions, allowing them to guide you to introspection and insight. Document your thoughts, experiences, and revelations, treating this journal as a confidant and a coach.

Commit to regular entries and revisit your responses periodically to get the maximum benefit. This will not only track your growth but also highlight areas for further development. Use the spaces provided to draft strategies, set goals, and articulate visions. Let this be a living document that grows with you, a testament to your journey in the art of leadership.

Consider pairing journaling sessions with strategic planning periods, team reviews, or personal reflection times to integrate these insights into actionable plans. Doing so ensures that the powerful play of leadership is not left on these pages but is brought to life in your daily practice.

1

RESILIENT LEADERSHIP

Adversity is an unforgiving teacher.
"Do not pray for an easy life; pray for the strength to endure a difficult one."
–Bruce Lee, Author of *The Warrior Within*

Without resilient leaders, it is impossible to create resilient teams. Resilient people are sometimes portrayed as fearless, unflappable individuals who are not readily affected by stress, failure, or setbacks. However, resilience is more than just "toughing it out." Being resilient includes more than simply being able to handle stress and strain.

During one of the most challenging periods of my career in a C-level position, I faced an ordeal that tested my resilience to its core. The year was marked not only by the high stakes of an election year but also by the global upheaval caused by the COVID-19 pandemic. Amidst this chaos, I endured a deeply personal tragedy that reshaped my perspective on leadership and resilience.

I lost two brothers within a short span, back-to-back. The pain of losing loved ones is always profound, but the circumstances were especially harrowing. As I was walking into the funeral for one brother, I received the devastating news that my other brother had passed away. In an instant, my grief was compounded, and I was thrust into the position of arranging another funeral, all while navigating the restrictions and risks of the pandemic.

During this time, I had to summon an extraordinary level of strength. With limited time to grieve, I organized the necessary arrangements and returned to my professional duties with unwavering determination. Despite the overwhelming sadness, I continued to travel and support my organization's efforts, refusing to let anything, not even a pandemic, hinder my commitment to success.

I was acutely aware that my colleagues and team members were also grappling with their own losses and challenges. I made a conscious decision to model resilience and strength in leadership. I wanted them to see that, even in the face of profound personal loss, it was possible to find the grace to acknowledge grief, work through it, and emerge with renewed determination. I showed up as best as I could, not only for myself but to reassure those around me that they were not alone in their struggles.

This experience taught me that true resilience is not just about enduring the physical and psychological demands of our roles but about embracing the intangibles—the unexpected challenges, the personal losses, and the inner battles. It is about showing up, day after day, with the resolve to keep moving forward, to lead by example, and to inspire those around us to do the same.

In sharing my story, I hope to illustrate that resilience in leadership is not just about being tough; it's about being human. It's about allowing ourselves to feel, to grieve, and to rise again, stronger and more compassionate, ready to face whatever comes next with unwavering resolve.

How do you bounce back from setbacks and lead your team through periods of uncertainty or adversity?

In today's corporate landscape, the capacity to withstand storms, adapt to challenges, and recover from setbacks is more essential than ever.

The need for resilience forms the foundation of successful leadership in every sector. Resilience gives leaders the tools they need to deal with ambiguity, adapt to change, and overcome obstacles head-on. Inspiring their team to overcome challenges and persist, a resilient leader not only looks after their own well-being but also sets an example for others.

Resilience in the face of difficulty promotes creative problem-solving, emotional stability, and the capacity to develop and learn from mistakes. In the landscape of contemporary leadership, it's not simply a characteristic but a lifeline that helps leaders stay steady and competent.

A scientific study on resilience research explored the complex interactions between psychological and neurological elements that allow people to overcome hardship. Cognitive adaptability, emotional regulation, and a positive attitude are the cornerstones of psychological resilience, which relates to the brain's capacity for neuronal rewiring and adaptation, with particular emphasis on areas such as the amygdala and prefrontal cortex.

Gaining an understanding of this science enables leaders to deliberately use these mechanisms. Leaders may proactively improve their resilience by developing cognitive and emotional skills and using neuroplasticity. To put it simply, leaders who understand the science of resilience are better equipped to strengthen their ability to flourish in the face of adversity.

1. Take lessons from misfortune.

Adversity may be a powerful teacher and motivator for human progress, as exemplified by Nelson Mandela, former President of South Africa. Despite facing enormous challenges and serving 27 years in jail, he came out of his experience with forgiveness, unflinching perseverance, and a vision for a better society. His capacity to draw lessons from misfortune, transform it into progress, and encourage peacemaking went beyond party lines.

Mandela's story emphasizes that obstacles do not have to define us; rather, they may make us stronger, more empathetic leaders. His lasting legacy serves as a reminder that adversity may spark extraordinary individual and collective development.

2. Assemble a leadership team with resilience.

Creating a resilient leadership team is essential to surviving today's fast-paced business climate. This entails cultivating an environment of open communication, trust, and cooperation. Team members should feel comfortable discussing challenges and failures, knowing they won't be judged. Fostering a growth mentality among team members enables them to see setbacks as chances for growth and development.

Setting an example of resilience and giving team members the tools and resources they need to overcome obstacles are important components of effective leadership. In such a setting, a resilient leadership team grows into a powerful force that can meet challenges head-on, come out stronger, and lead the company to victory.

3. Accept change as a chance.

Resilient leaders are characterized by their ability to view change as an opportunity for development and innovation rather than a threat. Through fostering an environment of adaptability and ongoing education, leaders motivate their groups to embrace change with zeal. This method encourages innovation, strengthens problem-solving skills, and advances businesses in a changing world.

Resilient leaders see the capacity to adapt and flourish in the face of change as a competitive advantage that sets up their teams and organizations for long-term success.

4. Techniques for Stress Management

Leaders must practice effective stress management to preserve their health and lead with clarity and poise. Stress-reduction techniques include deep-breathing exercises, mindfulness meditation, and regular physical activity.

Maintaining a balanced workload is made easier with the help of time management and prioritizing skills. Emotional tension can be reduced by asking for help and having honest conversations with peers or experts. Burnout may also be avoided by establishing firm limits and understanding when to say "no." Leaders must also refrain from perfectionism and engage in self-compassion.

Combined, these strategies help leaders effectively manage stress, strengthening their capacity to lead with resilience and concentration in trying circumstances.

5. Develop Resilience

Developing resilience in the face of setbacks is an essential leadership attribute. Resilient leaders see failure as a stepping stone to success rather than a dead end. They objectively assess defeats, draw conclusions, and modify their tactics. They retain a development mentality and persevere because they acknowledge that setbacks are an inevitable part of learning.

Resilience is strengthened through introspection and a dedication to ongoing development. Mentorship and support systems are essential for offering direction and inspiration. In the end, accepting failure as a worthwhile educational opportunity develops stronger, more adaptive leaders who are better able to overcome challenges and realize long-term successes.

Final Thoughts - Chapter 1

Resilience is a quality that can be developed and enhanced over time. Obstacles are only chances for you to improve. With the correct attitude and approaches, you can overcome setbacks and emerge stronger than before.

JOURNAL

How do you bounce back from setbacks and lead your team through periods of uncertainty or adversity?

_____

_____

_____

_____

_____

_____

_____

_____

_____

_____

_____

_____

_____

2

AUTHENTIC LEADERSHIP

"Authentic leaders are genuine in their intentions and understand the purpose of their leadership is serving their customers, employees, and investors, not their self-interest."
–Bill George, Author of *True North: Discover Your Authentic Leadership*

Authenticity is your leadership signature. Authentic leaders uphold high standards and integrity, and they act in the best interests of those they lead, which inevitably fosters trust and creates stronger teams.

Moreover, I want to go beyond the idea of authentic leadership and introduce you to what I refer to as respectful authenticity. At its core, this is about being true to yourself and acting in a way that is consistent with your values.

The idea of authenticity is not new.

I've added the term "respect" to help set it apart as a useful tool in business. By including the idea of respect, many of the drawbacks associated with simple authenticity are mitigated.

Being authentic does not necessarily mean simply speaking your mind or expressing your emotions. In fact, doing so might be detrimental to the organization as well as to you personally. You don't need to be an S.O.B. to be authentic. This type of attitude, "This is me, like it or not!" or "I'm upset, so

I'm entitled to shout at people," is something we've all encountered. Respectful authenticity, on the other hand, does not mean acting any way you like and showing little consideration for those around you.

The most effective authentic leaders communicate their truths with quiet confidence and sensitivity to the needs of others. This is a secret that they know, but others do not.

How does your team benefit from your true leadership style, and how do you exhibit it?

The attributes of a genuine leader must be understood before you can successfully respond to this question.

To effectively lead others, genuine leaders must first identify their purpose in leadership. Otherwise, they are at the whim of their egos and narcissistic tendencies. Genuine leaders must comprehend who they are and the passions that drive their life stories to find their mission.

The essential traits of real leaders are as follows:

1. Authentic leaders value humility, reflect on their actions, and present themselves in the best light.

"Never belittle someone unless you are assisting them in becoming better."[1] This Jesse Jackson quote exemplifies the need for humility in leadership. Humble people acknowledge that they can always improve, and you should urge your team members to do the same. This will allow them to develop and learn.

The capacity to understand who you are and what you stand for goes hand in hand with humility. This involves gaining an unbiased comprehension of your character, aspirations, driving forces, and strengths and weaknesses.

---

[1] https://www.britannica.com/biography/Jesse-Jackson

Leaders should ask open-minded colleagues for their candid opinions on their strengths and areas for development. When leaders incorporate this into their daily routine, they have a considerably higher chance of gaining the trust and allegiance of their team.

To make sure they are offering their best selves to their staff and have the energy to assist and mentor their team, leaders should emphasize self-care in addition to self-reflection.

2. Authentic leaders are empathetic and make a conscious effort to support and bring out the best in others.

Building relationships is the foundation of authentic leaders. Authentic leaders are ready to put themselves in other people's shoes and learn about their team members' personal and professional situations.

This strategy is about leading from your heart—that is, being more human while you lead. During the COVID pandemic and the turmoil that followed, I was always motivated to lead and speak with empathy and from my heart. There were days when the only thing on the schedule was to check in with the staff. In other instances, it was about expressing thanks and allowing staff to share their experiences, worries, and personal struggles while simultaneously managing my own.

In times of crisis, leaders who show empathy towards their staff and cultivate genuine connections and relationships are most effective in galvanizing their teams to effect positive change.

3. Authentic leaders are honest about possibilities and challenges.

Authentic leaders are aware that they must constantly explain the "why" behind their organizational initiatives to create real change and advance a company. This entails being open and honest about market possibilities and constraints, competition data, and how the vision relates to people.

Leaders must also respond to the question that all workers have during times of transition: "What's in it for me?" Once they are aware of the answer to this question, employees are significantly more likely to comprehend how they fit in and how they may contribute.

These are the three main things that workers expect to hear from their leaders, particularly during times of change, which is what business is all about these days:

- What the leaders are aware of and when they became aware of it.
- What the leaders are trying to learn but don't know.
- Information that is provided in an open, honest manner (don't sugarcoat it, and address any rumors or misconceptions that may be going around that aren't real).

4. Moral demands and standards are high among authentic leaders.

A strong moral compass is a trait of true leaders. They are concerned with leading their teams in the best possible way and advancing the company to meet the needs of the market, consumers, and the team as a whole.

Instead of just attempting to win over people or obtain something from them, authentic leaders act in a way that is consistent with their values.

The most important question you should always ask yourself as a leader striving for improvement is, "What would the best version of myself do?" To be an extraordinary leader, you must possess the courage to lead from both your heart and your brain.

5. Authentic leaders are great communicators and listeners.

Becoming an excellent communicator is crucial to becoming a great, genuine leader. The first step is giving your team members your whole attention. Leaders should, in general, listen much more than they speak.

In addition, leaders must take communication seriously. They should collaborate with a team of experts in the field who have a seat at the leadership table to develop strategies and a communication cadence that gives workers a "surround sound" experience. This involves using a range of engaging communication channels to ensure that team members receive information in the most convenient way.

Final Thoughts - Chapter 2

As we conclude this exploration of authentic leadership, remember that authenticity is not just a leadership style—it's your signature, defined by the respect you cultivate among your team. When leaders embrace authenticity, they create an environment where trust, transparency, and respect flourish. The true measure of your leadership lies in how your team benefits from your genuine approach and how you exhibit your leadership daily.

By valuing humility, reflecting on your actions, and consistently presenting your best self, you not only set a standard for your team but also inspire them to reach their full potential. Authentic leaders are empathetic, making a conscious effort to support others and bring out the best in them. They are honest about both possibilities and challenges, maintaining high moral standards and demanding excellence not just from their team but from themselves.

The ability for staff members to express their opinions, ask questions, and engage in conversation with leaders should be the top priority for leaders. When leaders foster such an environment, they do more than just manage a team—they create a motivated, empowered, and engaged workforce. This culture of open communication and mutual respect doesn't just benefit the team; it drives the entire organization toward success.

In embracing authentic leadership, you set the stage for greatness within your company. Your ability to lead with integrity, empathy, and respect will not only motivate your team but will also build a legacy of leadership that others will aspire to follow. This is the power of authenticity—leading in a way that is true to yourself and transformative for those you lead.

JOURNAL

In what ways do you demonstrate authenticity in your leadership style, and how does it impact your team?

_____

_____

_____

_____

_____

_____

_____

_____

_____

_____

_____

_____

_____

_____

How does your team benefit from your true leadership style, and how do you exhibit it?

_____

_____

_____

_____

_____

_____

_____

_____

_____

_____

_____

_____

_____

_____

3

ADAPTIVE LEADERSHIP

"Exercising adaptive leadership is about giving meaning
to your life beyond your own ambition."
–Ronald A. Heifetz, Author of *The Practice of Adaptive Leadership*

The only constant is change. In today's uncertain corporate environment, adaptability is essential for effective leaders. Such leaders can adapt their strategies to new difficulties that firms encounter, changing markets, and technological advancements. Those who possess adaptability can make judgments based on the facts of the moment, negotiate uncertainty with ease, and react quickly to new trends or crises.

Leadership Style

A leader's distinct set of attitudes, actions, and values that they display when dealing with their followers or team members is referred to as their leadership style. Their leadership philosophy, cultural background, experiences, and personality qualities are all reflected in it. A leader's style can impact organizational performance, work happiness, productivity, and employee motivation.

Leadership style serves as a framework for communicating expectations, making choices, and inspiring the group. Nevertheless, leaders must understand that no single approach is always successful. The most effective leaders are able to modify their approach in response to the demands of various circumstances, the requirements of their followers, and the objectives they want to accomplish.

How do you adapt your leadership approach in response to changing circumstances or unforeseen challenges?

Success in today's fast-paced and constantly evolving workforce requires competent leadership. Leaders must be able to adapt their leadership style to fit the demands of their team and company as the difficulties of the contemporary corporate environment continue to change. Having the flexibility and agility to lead is essential when dealing with new technology, evolving market situations, and changing consumer expectations.

Adapting Your Leadership Style

There is no one-size-fits-all solution in the ever-changing world of leadership. An effective leader must be able to modify their strategy to fit the needs of various circumstances.

This calls for a careful examination of several leadership philosophies and the ability to recognize which is best for any given situation. Leaders can maximize their effectiveness and get the best results by acknowledging that every circumstance is different and adapting their leadership style appropriately.

Circumstances Requiring Directive Leadership

In situations with precise job specifications, short deadlines, and urgent decision-making, directive leadership is required. A directed approach ensures effective execution and helps keep team members focused in high-pressure circumstances where time is limited or they lack experience.

This type of leadership involves giving clear directions, establishing clear expectations, and continuously monitoring development. To maintain control over the job at hand, leaders must strike a balance between being prescriptive and oppressive. They should create an atmosphere where team members feel empowered and driven.

Conditions Requiring Collaborative Leadership

Collaborative leadership thrives in environments where consensus-building, innovation, and teamwork are critical. By incorporating all members of the group in decision-making, leaders can effectively use the power of participation when dealing with complicated situations or when team members have differing opinions and experiences. Establishing a setting that promotes candid dialogue, attentive hearing, and ideation sessions increases team member involvement and makes better use of their combined knowledge to make decisions.

Conditions Requiring Delegative Leadership

When competent, motivated subordinates surround leaders, those leaders can afford to stand back and give team members more autonomy. This is especially true in situations where confidence has been built up within the team over time through successful delegation methods, such as detailed briefing meetings or explicit goal-setting. Leaders empower people and create a feeling of ownership and accountability by delegating responsibility and decision-making authority to the team, which encourages creativity and development.

Adaptability to Switch Between Several Styles

Excellent leaders are distinguished by their capacity to adapt their leadership style as circumstances change. They continuously evaluate the effectiveness of their selected leadership style because they understand that no circumstance is static.

Adapting Leadership and Management Style with Workforce Challenges

To meet the needs of the modern corporate landscape, let's examine three methods for realizing and adapting your leadership style:

1. Make sure your perception matches reality.

Managing a varied and dynamic staff is one of the main challenges facing today's corporate leaders. Leaders must first match their impression of the workforce with the reality of the situation to properly adapt their leadership style. This entails recognizing and appreciating the many requirements, values, and viewpoints that various groups—including those from different generations, ethnicities, and backgrounds—have inside the company.

Leaders must be willing to listen to and learn from their team members to match their perceptions with reality. This means asking for input, participating actively in discussions, and exhibiting an openness to comprehending and appreciating other viewpoints. By doing so, leaders can improve their comprehension of the challenges and possibilities confronting their workforce and create a leadership style that is more appropriate for the team's requirements.

An employer who understands that younger workers might have different expectations about work-life balance, for instance, is more inclined to provide remote work or flexible scheduling. In a similar vein, a boss who values diversity and inclusion would focus on developing an inclusive working environment that supports workers from all backgrounds and cultures. Ultimately, by aligning their perceptions with reality, leaders may forge closer bonds with their team members and foster a more productive and inclusive work environment. As a result, they will be better equipped to deal with the challenges of the contemporary business environment and propel their company to success.

2. Learn about your people.

Another important component is increasing your knowledge and familiarity with your personnel. Each person on your team has distinct qualities, shortcomings, motives, and communication styles. If you want to lead and manage your team effectively, you need to focus on your leadership development plan, recognize these individual distinctions, and adjust your approach appropriately.

One technique for getting to know your team is to hold regular one-on-one meetings. During these sessions, you can establish a connection with team members by discussing their objectives and challenges and giving them performance criticism. By listening to your team members' worries and suggestions, you can learn a lot about their motivations and success factors.

You may also use personality assessments and other tools to learn more about your team members' communication preferences, work styles, and personality qualities. With this understanding, you can modify your style of leadership to better suit each team member's requirements and tastes.

An extroverted team member might flourish in a collaborative and sociable work atmosphere, whereas an introverted team member would prefer written communication and explicit instructions. Your team members' demands will determine how best to adapt your leadership style to provide a more effective work atmosphere that encourages participation, creativity, and development.

It is crucial to get to know your people to adapt your leaders' style to the challenges of the contemporary corporate environment. By appreciating each team member's distinct contributions, you can improve relationships, boost motivation and engagement, and accomplish greater outcomes for your company.

3. Handle external pressures wisely.

It is also necessary to consider external influences that might affect your firm while adapting your leadership style to the challenges of the contemporary business environment. Changes in the political landscape, the state of the economy, and world events can significantly affect the performance of your team and the overall success of your firm. Leaders must be aware of these external forces and modify their strategies as necessary.

Creating backup plans that enable your company to react swiftly and efficiently to unforeseen developments is one way to consider external influences. For instance, you should have backup suppliers ready if your company depends significantly on a certain provider and the supply chain is disrupted. Similarly, you might need to stay abreast of changes to rules and regulations that could affect your business if your firm works in a highly regulated sector.

Apart from devising backup plans, it's critical to keep channels of communication open with all relevant parties, such as clients, investors, and staff. Maintaining communication with stakeholders about changes in the business environment and your organization's response can help you establish credibility and show that you are committed to openness and responsibility.

Last, but not least, it's critical to keep a fluid and adaptive leadership and management style that can react to shifting conditions. This might entail giving team members more decision-making power, keeping an open mind to fresh concepts and methods, and upholding a growth attitude that values trial and error and education.

Final Thoughts - Chapter 3

Now, I will ask again: how do you adapt your leadership approach in response to changing circumstances or unforeseen challenges?

JOURNAL

How do you adapt your leadership approach in response to changing circumstances or unforeseen challenges?

_____

_____

_____

_____

_____

_____

_____

_____

_____

_____

_____

_____

_____

4

ETHICAL LEADERSHIP

"Ethical leadership means doing the right thing
even when no one is watching."
–Unknown

Integrity is the cornerstone of trust. Ethical leaders practice appropriate behavior both within and outside the workplace. Their primary concerns are the formation of moral character and virtue. Through their words and deeds, ethical leaders demonstrate their values. They do not ignore wrongdoing even when doing so could be advantageous for their companies. Upholding morality and acting with integrity are at the core of being an ethical leader. Ethical leaders serve as role models for the rest of the organization.

How do you uphold ethical standards in your decision-making and actions?

Effective and responsible leaders must possess ethical leadership. This means exhibiting honesty, integrity, and a steadfast dedication to moral standards and values. In addition to making wise choices, ethical leaders foster loyalty, respect, and trust among their team members and stakeholders.

Here's a list of important traits and behaviors for ethical leaders:

1. Establish an ethical tone.

Moral leaders set the standard for the whole company. They create a climate of integrity, openness, and responsibility. Employees are encouraged to voice issues and support ethical standards in an atmosphere where ethical conduct and decision-making are routinely exhibited.

2. Maintain integrity in decision-making.

Ethical leaders base their choices on moral values rather than expediency or self-interest. They consider how their decisions will affect the organization, stakeholders, and society at large. Because of their dedication to honesty, those they lead will regard them more credibly and with integrity.

3. Model ethical behavior.

Setting a good example for followers is at the core of ethical leadership. Ethical leaders set an example for their team members by acting ethically. They promote an environment of respect for one another and common values by holding themselves to the same moral standards that they set for others.

4. Promote diversity and inclusivity.

Ethical leaders embrace diversity and inclusivity in the workplace. They aggressively seek feedback from a variety of voices and appreciate differing points of view. Leaders foster an inclusive atmosphere by promoting fairness and equal chances for everyone.

5. Encouraging ethical decision-making.

Ethical leaders motivate their staff to prioritize ethics when making decisions. To ensure that choices align with the organization's values, they facilitate candid conversations regarding moral conundrums and offer advice.

6. Communicate transparently.

Ethical leadership requires transparent communication. Even under trying circumstances, ethical leaders are forthright and honest with their team and stakeholders. Within the company, open communication promotes integrity and helps to establish trust.

7. Accept accountability.

Ethical leaders accept accountability for their deeds and choices, including any errors they may have made. Rather than assigning blame to others, they embrace mistakes as opportunities for growth and development.

8. Balance conflicting interests.

Ethical leaders consider the interests of all parties involved, such as the community, investors, staff, and clients. They constantly try to do what is right and fair, looking for solutions that balance conflicting interests.

9. Keep learning.

Ethical leaders must be dedicated to lifelong learning and personal development. Ethical leaders keep themselves updated on moral dilemmas and actively look for ways to broaden their knowledge of moral concepts and challenges.

10. Prioritize long-term sustainability.

Ethical leaders prioritize long-term sustainability in lieu of immediate profits. When making choices, they consider the organization, society, and environment.

Final Thoughts - Chapter 4

Ethical leaders must foster a healthy and enduring corporate culture. They engender trust, loyalty, and respect among their team members and stakeholders by modeling integrity, honesty, and a strong commitment to ethical principles and values. Ethical leaders create an example for others to follow and encourage inclusion, diversity, and openness inside the company. They place a high value on making moral decisions, owning up to their mistakes, embracing lifelong learning, and placing a strong emphasis on sustainability.

With moral leadership, organizations may flourish morally, have a positive effect on their communities, and improve the world.

JOURNAL

How do you uphold ethical standards in your decision-making and actions?

_____

_____

_____

_____

_____

_____

_____

_____

_____

_____

_____

_____

_____

5

VISIONARY LEADERSHIP

"The only thing worse than being blind is having sight but no vision."
–Helen Keller, Author and Disability Rights Activist

How can you envision the future to motivate action in the present? Reflect on your organization's future and your role as a storyteller of that vision. Everybody has seen leaders—in the media, their businesses, or even at work—whose leadership styles they like and want to emulate. These leaders seem to have a talent for inspiring and encouraging action and igniting change in teams and stakeholders. But what qualities do visionary leaders actually possess?

A visionary leader establishes a long-term vision, develops a plan of action to realize that vision, and enables others to work together to achieve that common objective.

Although senior-level managers at the top of the organizational structure are typically thought of as having leadership qualities, the reality is that managers' responsibilities frequently blur the lines between management and leadership (e.g., setting priorities and strategic planning) and involve daily operational direction.

To be a successful manager and inspire outstanding performance, you must develop the ability to adapt and adopt visionary leadership skills.

Furthermore, acquiring and exhibiting visionary leadership abilities might help you advance into senior management.

You can cultivate and display visionary leadership skills in the following ways:

1. Create a compelling vision.

For the team to function at its best and for you to carry out your job well, there must be a long-term end goal or vision. Managing everyday operations for a department that is not fixed-term can easily become just going through the motions. Programs and projects, on the other hand, often have set durations and a predetermined vision in place. Morale suffers as a result, and employees become disinterested in their work.

Defining an exciting vision will transform everything for you and your team. Collaborate with senior leadership teams to understand their overarching vision and strategy. Then, talk with them about distilling this vision into what is directly relevant to your and your team's roles.

This vision can't be limited to increasing profits. It must have global or societal significance. For instance, the goal of extending a health product's market reach may be to empower ten thousand people in that area to manage a particular component of their health.

2. Clearly articulate your vision.

Effective, convincing, self-assured, and inspiring communication is critical to visionary leaders' success. Use compelling storytelling to make the idea come to life and inspire your teams and stakeholders to act. Tell your teams that you have faith in their ability to succeed. You can also foster open communication by encouraging them to approach you with questions or concerns.

3. Accept change and adopt a growth mindset.

Being a visionary means being open to change and quickly adjusting to it. It can be easy to become mired in the notion that "this is how things are always done. Therefore, I won't do anything about it." However, to truly demonstrate leadership abilities, you must be prepared to advocate for a development mentality in your organization and encourage your subordinates, colleagues in management, and employers to embrace innovative and adaptable working practices.

4. Think creatively and take risks.

A deliberate attitude to accept risks, combined with a growth mentality, is a critical characteristic of a visionary leader. It encourages creativity and allows one to investigate topics that one may not have considered otherwise.

When taking a risk at work, weigh the advantages and disadvantages. Determine which factors are more important than the others, and then use your judgment, past performance, and knowledge of the risk to make an informed decision.

5. Consider the bigger picture.

Always remember that everything you do has long-term effects, as does everything your team does. Keep an eye on the broad picture and urge your team to consider how their effort will affect the community in the long run. You may excite and encourage your team while keeping the long-term goal in front of them by making the connections between their daily work and its overall impact and by helping them understand the necessity of interdepartmental communication.

Being a visionary does not mean you need to be a top-level manager. This week, start exhibiting visionary traits, and you'll see an improvement in team performance as well as increased prospects for job advancement. Though it takes time to develop the traits above, you may gradually become more and more like the visionary leaders you look up to.

What is your long-term vision for your organization, and how do you communicate it effectively to inspire others?

Now, let's break this down into smaller questions so you can get started easily.

Vistage speaker Luke Carlson argues that "looking around that corner" does not define a visionary leader.[2] Steve Jobs and Jeff Bezos, for example, are frequently seen as visionary leaders due to their ability to envision and develop technologies that society has come to depend on.

According to Carlson, the CEO and creator of Discover Strength in Minneapolis, Minnesota, visionary leadership is about more than just the leader.

Carlson stated, "We have the misconception that a visionary leader is someone who has fantastic ideas and understands where they want to go, but that's not what visionary leadership is." To this, he added, "An organization as a whole is inspired to share a vision by visionary leadership."

So, how might one go about fostering a common vision? According to Carlson, it all boils down to seven questions regardless of your goal, whether it's building a $1 million business or a $2 billion corporation. If every member of the company can comparably respond to these questions, you've established a common vision and shown visionary leadership.

1. What are your core values?

It should come as no surprise that a company should have core values, but visionary leaders run companies where all team members are aware of and consistent in their conduct with these values. A salesperson who takes phone

---

[2] http://lukecarlson.com/

calls from clients should be as proficient in reciting and explaining the company's values as a member of the C-suite.

But learning the values by heart is insufficient. If one of the organization's core values is continual learning, every employee should be able to show how the firm has given them opportunities to learn and improve over the last 90 days.

2. What is the core of your organization's existence?

What is the purpose of your organization other than generating revenue? The solution shouldn't be a goal or objective, nor should it have anything to do with technical proficiency. Why you think your organization exists in the first place should be the basis for your response. Of the seven questions, Carlson acknowledged that this one is sometimes the most difficult to respond to.

3. Which strategic niche do you fit into?

The response to this question ought to detail your company's source of revenue. Consider a group of sandboxes, each of which stands for a distinct industry or potential subindustry. Which sandbox does your company operate in? That specialization should be the source of all of your income. For instance, Southwest Airlines specializes in air travel. That's simple. It's not a straightforward solution for many leaders.

Understanding your specialty helps you avoid becoming sidetracked by shiny new things being produced in other sandboxes. In a similar vein, by identifying your specialty, you may direct your creativity and ideas to it rather than wasting time and money on unrelated endeavors.

4. What is your big, hairy, audacious goal (BHAG)?

A BHAG, as noted by Jim Collins in his book *Built to Last*, is a long-term, ambitious, and seemingly unachievable goal that serves to inspire and motivate an organization to reach for extraordinary success.

Answering the BHAG question should be the long-term objective of your company. In ten years, where do you want to be? The response needs to be focused, quantifiable, and ultimately related to your core goal. You should be able to confidently state after ten years that you've either achieved the objective or not. It doesn't matter if you succeed in reaching the objective; what matters is that you're moving in the correct path.

Your destination is the only thing you need to agree on when setting sail from Virginia into the Atlantic Ocean with a coworker. One person cannot be focused on getting to the Caribbean, and the other on thinking they are going to England.

If a team member is unaware of how their job fits into the organization's bigger goals, it will eventually make them disgruntled, and this can damage company culture. Becoming a bricklayer is one thing; actually laying the foundation for the Notre Dame Cathedral is another. A visionary leader is accountable for ensuring that all members of the organization are aware of their roles and the direction of the company.

5. What three-year plan do you have?

While the last question had an aspirational answer, this one requires a more specific response. What should your company's income and profit look like on this day three years from now? In addition to those quantifiables, think of four or five other crucial characteristics that may be evaluated beyond that three-year period to ascertain whether you've succeeded in your objective.

6. What's your one-year objective?

This question is more narrowly focused than the last since it's important to know what your objectives are for the upcoming year. According to Carlson, "Poor execution generally results from a lack of clarity around the purpose." Thus, everyone must be in agreement and know what their goals are for the year. Once more, establish goals for income, profit, and four or five supplementary factors that, when perfectly attained, will signify the accomplishment of the one-year objective.

7. What is your strategy?

Although there are many ways to understand strategy, according to Carlson, visionary leaders define it as their company's approach to standing out in a competitive market. Three strategic pillars that set your company apart—not better, but different—are the foundation of any winning plan. The crucial element is that your rivals must concur with your anchoring. It follows that you cannot claim to have better employees or provide better customer service than any other business. According to Carlson, while most entrepreneurs view things as excellent or fantastic, most customers don't share this perspective. They consider the differences. IKEA markets itself as different from other furniture companies, not as superior to them. The company does not deliver the furniture it sells. You assemble the furniture yourself using the parts provided, but it costs less than the products of the company's rivals. These are the strategic pillars that have helped IKEA become the most prosperous furniture store in the world.

Final Thoughts - Chapter 5

The power of your leadership lies not only in your ability to see the future but in your unwavering commitment to bringing that vision to life. It is your vision that will guide your organization through uncertainty, inspire innovation, and foster resilience. By reflecting on your core values and understanding the essence of your organization's existence, you lay the groundwork for a future that is not just aspirational but attainable. Embrace change, think creatively, and be willing to take calculated risks—these are the hallmarks of a visionary leader. As you chart your course, ensure that every step, from your big, hairy, audacious goal to your one-year objectives, aligns with the greater purpose you have set. In doing so, you will not only lead your organization toward success but also leave a lasting legacy that defines what true visionary leadership is all about.

JOURNAL

What is your long-term vision for your organization, and how do you communicate it effectively to inspire others?

_____

_____

_____

_____

_____

_____

_____

_____

_____

_____

_____

_____

_____

Which strategic pillars do you use? What distinguishes your business from its rivals?

_____

_____

_____

_____

_____

_____

_____

_____

_____

_____

_____

_____

_____

6

LEADING WITH PURPOSE

"Those who are able to inspire give people a sense of purpose or belonging that has little to do with any external incentive or benefit to be gained. Those who truly lead are able to create a following of people who act not because they were swayed, but because they were inspired."
–Simon Sinek, Author of *Find Your Why*

Purpose is the heartbeat of your organization. It is more crucial than ever to lead with purpose. Leaders with a sense of purpose are those who match the objectives of their companies and themselves with the greater good. Purpose-driven leaders motivate their teams to accomplish great things, improve society, and succeed in the long run.

Why Leading With Purpose Is Essential

1. Gives meaning and contentment.

For leaders and their teams, leading with purpose brings meaning and fulfillment. Teams and leaders are more likely to feel fulfilled and satisfied with their jobs when they are contributing to the greater good. This results in improved productivity and general performance, as well as a happier workplace.

2. Builds a closer link with stakeholders and customers.

Lead with a goal in mind to strengthen relationships with stakeholders and customers. It is simpler to communicate a company's values and goals to people when it has a clear sense of purpose. As a result, the company's customer base grows more devoted, and new clients who share the company's values are drawn in.

3. Promotes long-term success.

Leaders who lead with purpose are also more likely to succeed over the long run. Purpose-driven leaders foster an environment of excellence where staff members are inspired to perform to the best of their abilities. This results in better retention rates, improved productivity, and, eventually, larger revenues.

How do you align your leadership actions with the core purpose and values of your organization?

A leader's job is not only to direct their team but also to continuously improve their team members. While balancing the demands of their company, leaders with a purpose put the needs of their people, clients, and community first. Although it's difficult, it's worthwhile to link your job to a greater sense of purpose since it improves performance, gives you more energy, and makes it easier for you to enter a learning state.

1. Define your purpose.

Identifying your mission is the first step toward being a purpose-driven leader. What motivates you? Which values and beliefs do you hold? If you have a firm understanding of your mission, you can align your objectives and behaviors with your greater purpose.

2. Communicate your purpose.

It's critical to communicate your objective to your team after you've established it. This fosters motivation and a sense of alignment with a shared objective. Communicate your mission succinctly and clearly to ensure that your staff understands it.

3. Match your behavior to your purpose.

Purpose-driven leaders must match their behaviors to their goals. This means making choices consistent with one's values and beliefs. It also entails fostering an environment of excellence where your staff members are inspired to perform to the best of their abilities.

4. Strengthen your team.

A leader with a clear mission empowers their group. This requires providing your staff with the tools necessary for success as well as chances for personal development. It also entails establishing a safe work atmosphere where members of your team are encouraged to attempt new things and take calculated risks.

5. Assess your influence.

It's critical to gauge your influence. Establish objectives and key performance indicators (KPIs) that are consistent with your mission. Then, monitor your advancement toward them. This will guarantee that you are contributing positively to society and help you stay focused on your goal.

Final Thoughts - Chapter 6

In the corporate environment, leading with purpose is not just a preference—it's a necessity. A purpose-driven leader is someone who not only understands the mission of the organization but also embodies it in every decision, action, and interaction. To become such a leader, you must first define your mission clearly, ensuring that it resonates with your core values and aligns with the long-term goals of your organization. This mission should be more than just words on a page; it should be a guiding force that shapes your leadership style and influences every aspect of your work.

Once your mission is defined, the next critical step is to communicate it effectively to your team. A clear and compelling mission can inspire and motivate your team, giving them a sense of direction and purpose. This communication should be ongoing, reinforcing the mission in daily operations and meetings, and through the example you set as a leader.

Leading with purpose also means matching your actions to your mission. Your team will look to you as a role model, so it's essential that your decisions and behavior consistently reflect the values and objectives you've set. This alignment builds trust and credibility, reinforcing your commitment to the mission and encouraging your team to do the same.

Empowering your team is another key aspect of purpose-driven leadership. By giving your team members the tools, resources, and autonomy they need to contribute to the mission, you foster a sense of ownership and engagement. When people feel connected to a higher purpose and know that their work is meaningful, they are more likely to go above and beyond to achieve collective goals.

Finally, to truly lead with purpose, you must regularly assess your influence and impact. This involves not only evaluating the success of your team and the organization in meeting its objectives but also reflecting on how well you've stayed true to your mission. Are you leading with integrity and consistency? Is your team aligned with the purpose you've communicated? By continually reassessing and adjusting your approach, you ensure that your leadership remains purpose-driven, adaptable, and effective.

Adhering to these principles will not only help you become a purpose-driven leader but also position you to achieve significant and sustainable success. In a world where purpose is increasingly recognized as a key driver of organizational performance, leading with a clear, communicated, and actionable mission can set you and your team apart in the pursuit of greatness.

JOURNAL

How do you align your leadership actions with the core purpose and values of your organization?

_____

_____

_____

_____

_____

_____

_____

_____

_____

_____

_____

_____

_____

7

LEADING BY EXAMPLE

"Become the kind of leader that people would follow voluntarily;
even if you had no title or position."
–Brian Tracy, Author of *No Excuses!*

Actions speak volumes.

Setting an example via deeds and behaviors that encourage and inspire others, and not merely telling people what to do, is a key component of leadership. Building trust, cultivating a supportive culture, and establishing a feeling of purpose among team members are all achieved when leaders exhibit positive behaviors. Your obligations to your team's growth expand along with your leadership responsibilities.

Leaders who set an example for their followers bring about positive change. It is easier for people to follow leaders who exhibit the behaviors they want from their team, which builds trust and credibility.

A strong team is largely dependent on the stability and dependability that leaders foster via their words and deeds. Setting a good example can contribute to the development of a positive culture and establish credibility and trust.

Leaders who exhibit positive actions and attitudes foster an upbeat and optimistic culture that can increase team members' motivation and sense of engagement. Positive and encouraging leaders increase the likelihood that their team members will feel valued and appreciated, which can boost morale and output.

How do you model the behaviors and values you expect from your team members as a leader?

Team members feel a sense of purpose when they see their leaders leading by example. When leaders exhibit the behaviors and values that are significant to the company, team members are better able to understand what is required of them and what the corporation stands for. This can inspire them to collaborate to achieve common objectives.

It's not always simple to lead by example, but it's crucial for good leaders. Leaders can set an example for followers in the following ways:

1. Adopt an open and honest attitude.

It's not as simple as it sounds. Transparent and open leaders promote a culture of trust and honesty. Leaders can foster trust with their team members by being transparent and honest when delivering facts.

2. Be professional and courteous.

Respect must be earned. Courteous and professional leaders create a healthy culture of respect and professionalism. The organization's leaders are the first to set the standard for decency and professionalism. Leaders show their importance and appreciation for the team and each member's contributions when they treat all team members with respect.

3. Establish high standards.

Leaders who hold themselves and their team members to a high level show they are dedicated to excellence. Leaders can motivate their teams to pursue greatness by establishing high standards.

4. Be accountable.

Leaders who hold themselves accountable for their errors foster a culture of accountability. Leaders demonstrate their dedication to ongoing development when they acknowledge their mistakes and take the necessary corrective action.

Final Thoughts - Chapter 7

Lead by example by paying attention to your team members' thoughts and ideas. A culture of cooperation and open communication may be fostered by leaders who are good listeners.

Effective leaders must lead by example. Building a healthy culture, trust, and a feeling of shared purpose among team members are all facilitated by leaders who set an example of positive actions and attitudes. Leaders may foster a culture of excellence and continuous development by modeling the behaviors they demand from their team members, being open, honest, polite, and professional, establishing high expectations, being accountable, and practicing active listening.

JOURNAL

How do you model the behaviors and values you expect from your team members as a leader?

_____

_____

_____

_____

_____

_____

_____

_____

_____

_____

_____

_____

_____

_____

8

LEADING WITH INTEGRITY

*"Integrity is the most valuable and respected quality of leadership.
Always keep your word."*
–Brian Tracy, Author of *Million Dollar Habits*

Integrity is non-negotiable. We are free to choose how the world perceives us, who we are, and what we want to become. I often glance at social media to see how society is changing—or, in many cases, deteriorating—and to see what kinds of habits are influencing our actions. To what extent is this conduct being transferred to the workplace?

People will publish anything, and I mean anything, to gain attention, which astounds me. Please understand, however, that there is genuine value on the internet.

In a society full of scandals and moral failings, leaders who uphold integrity have emerged as a source of inspiration and hope. Integrity in leadership is not only a positive character trait; it is the cornerstone of loyalty, trust, and sustained success.

We need leaders and independent contributors with integrity, as they can have a significant impact on people, organizations, and society at large.

Integrity is characterized by honesty, trustworthiness, and moral rectitude. It also includes living by a strict code of morality and ethics, acting consistently with one's beliefs, and feeling strongly accountable to oneself and other people. Integrity-driven leaders make decisions based on what is right rather than what is convenient and continually connect their actions with their principles.

How do you uphold ethical standards and integrity in your leadership role?

Leadership with integrity has a profound impact on both people and institutions. When leaders regularly model honesty, openness, and ethical decision-making, they maintain a culture of trust and credibility among their teams. This enhances worker satisfaction and motivation, cultivating a more efficient and amicable workplace.

Beyond the workplace, leaders with integrity inspire people to embrace ethical ideals by acting as role models for their communities and society at large. As integrity in leadership establishes a high standard for behavior and inspires others to follow suit, it also makes the world a more equitable and ethical place. This has a beneficial and long-lasting effect on both organizational and societal levels.

Loyalty and Trust

Integrity-driven leaders engender trust in their followers. Leaders who continuously exhibit honesty, openness, and dependability foster a sense of security and loyalty. Strong connections are built, which helps teams work together productively and produce amazing outcomes.

Leadership with integrity shapes the company culture and values. Its leaders' activities and behaviors shape the organization as a whole. They encourage staff to maintain the highest moral standards by prioritizing integrity and creating a motivated, safe, and secure workplace.

Reputation and Brand Image

Leaders who uphold integrity improve their businesses' reputation and brand image. Customers, stockholders, and the general public respect and admire leaders who operate with integrity in this age of increased public scrutiny and social media impact. This raises the organization's competitiveness and draws in skilled people.

Final Thoughts - Chapter 8

Leaders with integrity can be agents of positive change in society. They encourage others to follow their lead by acting morally and speaking up against injustice, corruption, and unethical behavior. They help to shape a future based on integrity, making the world more just and sustainable.

JOURNAL

How do you uphold ethical standards and integrity in all aspects of your leadership role?

_____

_____

_____

_____

_____

_____

_____

_____

_____

_____

_____

_____

_____

_____

_____

9

LEADING WITH EMPATHY

"Empathy is not just about understanding others,
it's about understanding yourself."
–Brené Brown, Author of *Dare to Lead*

E mpathy is the soul of connection. It is crucial for leaders to exhibit empathy to build connections and trust among their workforce. Better communication results from demonstrating empathy, which is the capacity to understand and share the emotions of others with kindness and wisdom.

The capacity to sense and comprehend the feelings of others is a critical quality for leaders. It entails putting oneself in another's shoes, making an effort to comprehend their perspective, and responding with understanding and care.

An empathetic leader cultivates strong bonds with others, gains their trust, and fosters a happy workplace. Additionally, empathy in a leader facilitates better team member communication, awareness of their needs, and the ability to make well-informed decisions that are best for the group and the company.

How do you demonstrate empathy and understanding towards your team members' perspectives and experiences?

Effective leadership goes beyond overseeing projects and groups in today's complicated and often-changing world. Empathy is one of the most critical characteristics of exceptional leaders, a fundamental attribute that promotes trust, teamwork, and a healthy company culture. It is not merely a desirable feature for leaders.

1. Actively listen.

Engage in active listening by paying close attention to what your teammates say. Refrain from interjecting, and feel free to ask clarifying questions to ensure you comprehend their viewpoints.

2. Put yourself in your teammates' shoes.

Make an effort to understand circumstances from your teammates' perspectives. When making decisions or giving feedback, consider their motives, feelings, and obstacles.

3. Establish open communication.

Establish a setting where communication is transparent and open. Encourage team members to voice their opinions, worries, and ideas without worrying about criticism.

4. Express gratitude.

Acknowledge and value the work and contributions that your team members have made. Saying "thank you" can be a very effective way to express your gratitude and empathy.

5. Provide support.

Stand by your teammates when they face difficulties.

6. Offer growth opportunities.

Recognize the professional goals and aspirations of your team members and help them hone their abilities and achieve their objectives. This demonstrates your concern for their career development.

7. Own up to errors.

Leaders make mistakes. Admit your mistakes honestly and accept responsibility for them. This exemplifies vulnerability and accountability.

Final Thoughts - Chapter 9

Leading with empathy is not just about understanding your team members; it's about actively engaging with their experiences and perspectives. By actively listening and putting yourself in their shoes, you foster a culture of openness and trust. Establishing open communication, expressing gratitude, and providing support create an environment where team members feel valued and motivated. Offering growth opportunities shows your commitment to their development, and owning up to errors demonstrates integrity and humility. Ultimately, embodying empathy in your leadership approach ensures a positive, inclusive, and productive workplace. Remember, leading with empathy means prioritizing humanity and respect with every interaction.

JOURNAL

How do you demonstrate empathy and understanding towards your team members' perspectives and experiences?

_____

_____

_____

_____

_____

_____

_____

_____

_____

_____

_____

_____

_____

10

STRATEGIC THINKING

"Strategy is a style of thinking, a conscious and deliberate process, an intensive implementation system, the science of ensuring future success."
–Pete Johnson, Author

S trategic thinking is a tapestry woven with threads of insight, foresight, and hindsight. In the dynamic corporate landscape of 2024, leaders will find strategic thinking and decision-making to be essential competencies. Understanding the wider picture, foreseeing future trends, and making decisions that align with long-term goals are all part of these talents, in addition to making daily decisions.

Strategic decision-making entails adopting a comprehensive, long-term approach that considers the big picture and the potential effects of decisions in the future. It involves comprehending the complex relationships between the company, market, and larger environment.

On the other hand, decision-making is the process of selecting the optimal course of action from a range of options. Leaders are typically required to balance short-term operational demands with long-term strategic goals.

How do you cultivate a strategic mindset and think long-term in your decision-making processes?

A strategic mindset is essential for making decisions in difficult and unclear circumstances. A strategic mindset enables you to look beyond the present possibilities and difficulties and foresee your decisions' long-term effects and ramifications. It also helps you adjust to changing conditions and make decisions that are consistent with your vision, purpose, and goals.

How can one develop a strategic mindset outside of the current circumstance? To improve your capacity for strategic thinking, consider the following list of effective strategies:

1. Ask "why" and "what if."

By asking yourself "why" and "what if" questions, you cultivate a strategic mindset with one of the easiest and most effective methods possible. What is the reason for your actions? Why are you going with one choice instead of another? Why are you adhering to this protocol or process? What if you take a different action? What happens if anything changes? What happens if your resources change?

You may better understand your goals, test your presumptions, consider other options, and foresee scenarios by using why and what if questions. It also helps prevent prejudice, routine, and habitual behavior.

2. Look for other viewpoints.

Seeking out other viewpoints from various sources is another method to cultivate a strategic mindset. This can include external stakeholders, clients, rival businesses, or subject matter experts, as well as people with varying backgrounds, specializations, responsibilities, or organizational levels.

By seeking out different viewpoints, you avoid groupthink, learn from others, and expand your views and ideas. Additionally, it enables you to balance various demands, expectations, and interests when making decisions by fostering empathy for them.

3. Think in systems.

Thinking in systems as opposed to silos is a third strategy for cultivating a strategic mindset. A system comprises several interconnected parts that affect the total and each other. Understanding the overall picture, the underlying causes, the feedback loops, and the leverage points in a situation are all made easier by thinking in terms of systems. It also helps you determine the trade-offs, unexpected repercussions, synergies, and interdependencies between your decisions. You may avoid oversimplifying, disregarding, or stumbling over significant linkages or elements by adopting a systems-thinking mindset.

4. Learn from your mistakes.

Experimenting and learning from your decisions and results is a fourth technique for cultivating a strategic mindset. Experimentation includes trying new things, verifying theories, and taking measured risks. Learning involves evaluating your experiences, interpreting your findings, and putting what you've learned into practice.

You must experiment and learn to innovate, improve, and adapt to changing circumstances. This also helps with progress measurement, course correction, and assumption validation or invalidation.

5. Seek feedback and mentorship.

Seeking mentoring and feedback from others is a fifth method for cultivating a strategic mindset. Requesting and accepting constructive criticism, compliments, or recommendations from others is known as feedback. To be mentored is to seek out and follow a person who can coach, lead, or advise you on your personal development.

By asking for feedback and seeking guidance, you may develop awareness, self-assurance, and drive in your strategic thinking abilities. You may also learn from other people's failures, experiences, and best practices.

6. Review and revise.

The sixth technique for cultivating a strategic mindset is regularly reviewing and revising your decisions and activities. Reviewing entails comparing your performance, results, and effects to your goals, standards, and anticipations. To revise, you must update, alter, or change your decisions and actions in light of your review.

Making necessary revisions and reviews to your strategic thinking will help guarantee its coherence, efficacy, and alignment. Acknowledging your accomplishments, obstacles, and room for growth is also beneficial.

Final Thoughts - Chapter 10

Many believe that strategic thinking is an innate talent, but research and practical experience show that it is a skill that can be developed. According to the Center for Creative Leadership (CCL), strategic thinking involves the ability to anticipate, challenge, interpret, decide, align, and learn. CCL's research indicates that while some individuals may naturally possess these abilities, most can cultivate them through deliberate practice and development.

Harvard Business Review also supports this view, highlighting that strategic thinking can be nurtured through specific practices such as exposing oneself to diverse perspectives, seeking out challenging assignments, and engaging in reflective thinking. They suggest that with the right mindset and tools, anyone can enhance their strategic thinking capabilities.

Expanding on this, the process of becoming a strategic thinker involves consistently asking probing questions, seeking varied viewpoints, thinking in systems, learning from mistakes, and actively seeking feedback and mentorship. Regularly reviewing and revising one's approach further strengthens this skill. This conscious effort and commitment to growth enable individuals to transform into effective strategic thinkers, regardless of their starting point.

JOURNAL

How do you cultivate a strategic mindset and think long-term in your decision-making processes?

_____

_____

_____

_____

_____

_____

_____

_____

_____

_____

_____

_____

_____

_____

11

STRATEGIC PLANNING

"Success is 20% skills and 80% strategy. You might know how to succeed,
but more importantly, what's your plan to succeed?"
–Jim Rohn

The blueprint of success begins with a plan.

Most bigger firms frequently prepare for the future every three to five years. Documents related to strategic planning are frequently put on a shelf and ignored until the next cycle starts. However, driven by a sense of urgency, a lot of smaller and more recent firms might not invest the required time and effort in the strategic planning process.

Only 63% of companies make plans that extend beyond a year. They overlook the fact that settling for "any route" might not lead them to where they want to go, despite what Alice is told in her encounter with the Cheshire Cat in *Alice in Wonderland*.

All businesses must have a more thorough yearly planning process if they want to drive future success, profitability, value, and impact. As notable innovation expert and former Harvard Business School professor John Kotter argues, "Strategy should be understood as a dynamic force that continuously finds opportunities, creates initiatives that will capitalize on them, and completes those projects rapidly and effectively."[3]

---

[3] https://www.betterup.com/blog/strategic-planning

Strategic planning is a continuous process that helps an organization establish its future direction. It involves bringing together all of its stakeholders to assess the business's current state and define its goals for the future.

It examines its advantages, disadvantages, and accessible resources. Strategic planning aims to foresee emerging market trends. Throughout the process, the company develops a vision, clarifies its mission, and establishes long-term, forward-looking strategic goals.

Those strategic goals determine operational objectives and necessary incremental milestones. The operational plan has well-defined goals and corresponding efforts connected to metrics that all parties are responsible for meeting. The strategy should be flexible enough to accommodate resource redistribution in response to internal and external factors and required recalibrations.

How do you set strategic goals, develop action plans, and track progress towards achieving them?

Although developing a strategy requires a lot of work, the rewards are long-lasting. The adage "If you fail to plan, you plan to fail" applies after all.

1. Explain your goal and vision.

State the organization's future vision at the outset. Ask, "In five years, what does success look like?" Make a mission statement that outlines your organization's values and your plan for achieving the vision. What values guide and define the purpose, vision, and mission?

The "why" of the company's actions is communicated through purpose-driven strategic goals. By connecting the vision statement to particular goals, the company establishes a link between the bigger picture and the work that teams and individuals do.

2. Carry out an exhaustive evaluation.

Determining an organization's strategic stance is part of this step.

At this point, information is gathered from the relevant stakeholders as well as from the internal and external surroundings, including clients and staff.

The assignment is to do research to compile market statistics. One of the most important parts of this phase is a thorough SWOT analysis, which entails assembling participants and incorporating viewpoints from all parties involved to ascertain:

- Strengths
- Weaknesses
- Opportunities
- Threats

First, planners pinpoint the company's assets that support its present competitive advantage and/or the possibility of a substantial future market share gain. This should not be an exaggerated view of its advantages but an impartial appraisal.

To assess vulnerabilities accurately, it is necessary to look at external influences that might lead to either fresh possibilities or dangers. Think about the significant changes in several companies whose plans were thrown off by the COVID-19 epidemic. Tech businesses were able to take advantage of the situation and meet the needs of remote work, but it was devastating for the business models of the restaurant and airline sectors.

3. Forecast.

Use financial forecasting to ascertain the company's worth, taking the aspects above into account. Even though the five factors will most likely cause it to change, a forecast can identify the first quantifiable outcomes predicted in the plan, such as return on investment (ROI).

4. Establish the business's organizational orientation.

The research and evaluation mentioned above can help set objectives and goals for a company. An organization's strategic plan is often overly expansive and ambitious. Planners must ask themselves, "What type of influence are we attempting to have, and in what time frame?" They must focus on the goals that will have the biggest influence.

5. Establish strategic goals.

The next stage of operational planning is developing strategic goals and initiatives. Robert S. Kaplan (an accounting academic and Harvard leadership professor) and David P. Norton (business theorist and management consultant) are the co-creators of a 1992 Harvard Business Review article, "The Balanced Scorecard: Measures That Drive Performance," a strategic planning and management framework that helps organizations translate their vision and strategy into action across four perspectives. In their balanced scorecard technique, Kaplan and Norton propose that these four viewpoints should be considered to determine the conditions for success. Since they are connected, they must be assessed simultaneously.

- **Monetary:** Strategic efforts are informed by factors such as enhancing shareholder value, boosting revenue, controlling expenses, enhancing profitability, or maintaining financial security.

- **Customer Satisfaction:** Goals can be ascertained by defining benchmarks pertaining to any or all of the following: best service, value for money, growing market share, or offering consumers solutions.

- **Internal Procedures:** These include improving workplace safety, cutting costs, investing in innovation, investing in complete quality and performance management, optimizing operational procedures and efficiency, or simplifying procedures.

- **Learning and Growth:** To maintain change, organizations need to consider whether they have implemented initiatives related to human capital, learning, and growth. Goals might include developing high-performing teams, keeping employees happy, increasing productivity, or laying the groundwork for future leaders.

6. Align with key stakeholders.

Teamwork is required. The degree to which the business is willing to inform and include every employee in the strategy's implementation will determine how well the plan works. Only when a plan is linked to the objectives of the company will people be dedicated to seeing it through to completion. When all parties are working towards the same goal, cross-functional decision-making becomes more seamless and coordinated.

7. Get your strategy mapping started.

A strategy map is an effective tool for linking viewpoints to strategic objectives. It shows the cause-and-effect relationship between those perspectives. The map offers an understandable graphic for all company members to create common knowledge at all levels, as most people learn best visually.

8. Determine strategic initiatives.

Once strategic objectives have been developed, strategic initiatives are chosen. These include things like scope, budget, developing new products, increasing brand recognition, and staff training.

9. Benchmark performance metrics and their interpretation.

Metrics are allocated to SMART goals to assess performance, which are informed by strategic efforts. Senior management implements these policies, which then trickle down to front-line employees. Determining the operational strategy requires establishing objectives that are precise, quantifiable, reachable, pertinent, and time-bound.

A calendar is constructed, and benchmarks are set against which performance may be measured. Organizational goals determine the assignment of KPIs. These metrics match employee productivity and performance with long-term strategic goals.

10. Assess the Performance.

Evaluating a plan's effectiveness by tracking actions and advancement toward goals enables the development of better plans and goals to raise performance levels.

Final Thoughts - Chapter 11

Consider the process of strategic planning as a circle that starts and ends with assessment. Modify a strategy as needed. For many firms, the strategy has to be reviewed annually; for those in quickly changing sectors, it may need to be reviewed every three months.

JOURNAL

How do you set strategic goals, develop action plans, and track progress towards achieving them?

_____

_____

_____

_____

_____

_____

_____

_____

_____

_____

_____

_____

_____

_____

12

STRATEGIC COMMUNICATION

"Take advantage of every opportunity to practice your communication skills
so that when important occasions arise, you will have the gift, the style,
the sharpness, the clarity, and the emotions to affect other people."
–Jim Rohn, Author of *The Art of Exceptional Living*

Communication is your bridge to connection.

As a leader, you have a vision and goals for your team, but how can you successfully communicate them? How do you lead, encourage, and synchronize your team members with your objectives and direction? Your communication skills, which are among the most crucial skills for leaders, can be made or broken by your team's performance and morale.

What is leadership communication?

Leadership communication is the process of informing, motivating, and inspiring your team to work toward shared objectives by conveying information about the business, its processes, and its culture. The following aspects of your workplace can be improved by having clear communication with your team:

- **Arrangement of Parts:** It is simpler for your staff to grasp what you want from them when you communicate your expectations clearly, allowing them to behave in accordance with your preferences. Roles and responsibilities may be clearly understood thanks to this well-run organization.

- **Emotional Security:** Your leadership communication skills enable you to connect with and develop trust with your team. As a result, your team members will be more likely to trust one another and feel free to share their thoughts.

- **Team Unity:** Effective communication keeps all staff members working toward the same general objective for smoother integration, especially when managing teams or individuals working on different but connected tasks. Additionally, it can provide a sense of unity and support for the work that each team is doing.

How do you ensure your communication is clear, consistent, and aligned with your leadership goals?

For a leader, communication is a fundamental talent, and you can keep your team members happy by continuously improving your communication. This may result in the best possible team productivity, which benefits the company, you, and your teammates. The following actions can help you enhance your leadership communication and gauge its effectiveness:

- **Consider yourself.** Assessing your performance as a leader is the first step towards identifying your challenges and strengths. Finish your self-evaluation by considering measurements, personal observations, and the criticism you've received.

- **Determine what needs improvement.** Once your evaluation is complete, review your results and note any communication gaps that need to be filled. When evaluating your strengths, consider using them as standards.

- **Make a plan for development.** Once you've recognized your communication challenges, you may create a strategy to overcome them. Establishing SMART goals—Specific, Measurable, Achievable, Relevant, and Time-bound—might be beneficial.

- **Monitor your development.** Make a written record of your objective progress using a spreadsheet or document. Add a few targets and set deadlines for tracking your advancement till you accomplish them.

- **Carry out this procedure on a regular basis.** Continuous improvement is necessary for professional development and successful leadership. By doing this, you can continue to assess how well your communication and other skills are working.

Final Thoughts - Chapter 12

As we wrap up this chapter on strategic communications, it's essential to remember that communication is not just a tool for transmitting information—it's the bridge that connects you to your team, aligning them with your vision and goals. As a leader, your ability to communicate effectively is paramount, influencing everything from team morale to performance. Leadership communication goes beyond mere words; it's about informing, motivating, and inspiring your team to work together toward shared objectives.

Effective communication clarifies roles and responsibilities, fosters emotional security, and unites your team with a common purpose. When you communicate clearly and consistently, you create an environment where your team understands your expectations and feels empowered to meet them. This, in turn, strengthens the organization and enhances overall productivity.

Improving your leadership communication is an ongoing process that requires reflection, evaluation, and a commitment to growth. By continuously assessing and refining your communication strategies, you ensure that your team remains motivated, aligned, and capable of achieving the goals you've set. Remember, great leaders are also great communicators, and by mastering this skill, you not only guide your team but also cultivate a culture of trust, collaboration, and excellence within your organization.

JOURNAL

How do you ensure your communication is clear, consistent, and aligned with your leadership goals?

_____

_____

_____

_____

_____

_____

_____

_____

_____

_____

_____

_____

_____

_____

13

STRATEGIC RESOURCE ALLOCATION

"Doing more of what doesn't work won't make it work any better."
–Charles J. Givens, Author of *Wealth Without Risk*

Resources are finite.

The process of defining an organization's long-term goals and objectives and creating the most effective plans to attain them is known as strategic planning. Allocating resources entails choosing how to divide the time, funds, people, and other resources among the multitude of projects and activities that support the organization's plan. This is a crucial part of strategic planning. An organization may maximize performance, impact, and efficiency while minimizing waste, duplication, and conflict by allocating resources effectively.

How do you allocate resources strategically to maximize efficiency and effectiveness within your organization?

A key component of creating and carrying out strategic action plans is allocating resources. The time, money, people, equipment, and materials required to fulfill the plan's goals and objectives are referred to as resources. You must prioritize and make the best use of your resources because they are frequently few, limited, or competing.

1. Match resources to the big picture.

The first step is ensuring that your resources align with your vision, purpose, and values. You need to devote resources to endeavors and initiatives that uphold your strategic orientation and objectives. Your strategic priorities and goals can be identified and assessed using techniques like a balanced scorecard, strategy map, and SWOT analysis. After that, you may distribute resources based on their significance, immediacy, and practicability.

2. Evaluate the capacity and availability of resources.

The next stage is to evaluate the availability and capability of your resources, both present and future. You should assess the quantity and kind of resources you have or can access, as well as the extent to which they can carry out the operations and duties stipulated in the plan. To manage and keep an eye on your resource availability and demand, you may use tools like a resource inventory, resource calendar, or resource breakdown structure. Then, you can find any shortages, excesses, or restrictions that can influence how you allocate your resources.

3. Maximize the use of resources.

The third phase is optimizing the way you use your resources. This means that you ought to distribute resources in a manner that optimizes their efficacy, value, and efficiency. A resource allocation matrix, a resource leveling approach, or resource optimization software are some examples of tools that you may use to distribute resources according to their appropriateness, cost, availability, and quality. The trade-offs between allocating resources and the project's scope, timeline, and budget may then be balanced.

4. Communicate and work together.

Working together and communicating with your stakeholders is the fourth phase. You must provide information about your resource allocation decisions and procedures with your partners, customers, suppliers, managers, and team members. To successfully communicate and interact, you might use tools like a feedback system, stakeholder analysis, or communication plan. You can then build trust, transparency, and responsibility for the distribution of your resources.

5. Keep an eye on resources and make adjustments.

Monitoring and modifying your resource allocation is the last phase. This means that you assess and gauge the performance of your resources in relation to the goals and metrics of your strategy. You can track and modify how you allocate your resources by using tools such as a dashboard, report, or review meeting. Any problems, risks, or changes that might have an impact on your resource allocation can be found and addressed.

Final Thoughts - Chapter 13

You may deploy resources in strategic action plans critically and methodically by implementing these strategies. Along with this, you will sharpen your strategic thinking and resource management skills.

JOURNAL

How do you allocate resources strategically to maximize efficiency and effectiveness within your organization?

_____

_____

_____

_____

_____

_____

_____

_____

_____

_____

_____

_____

_____

_____

14

STRATEGIC PARTNERSHIPS

*"Strategic partnerships can be a major source of competitive advantage,
enabling companies to achieve things they couldn't on their own."*
–Michael Porter, business theorist, author and scholar

P artnerships can amplify impact.

Leading small companies requires enterprises to find new methods of standing out from the competition and expanding their market share. For the benefit of the small company ecosystem and large organizations' ability to increase their income, businesses must innovate successfully and provide the goods and services that small business owners require.

Strategic partnerships are a highly successful strategy for organizations that deal with small and medium-sized businesses to boost their commercial perspective. The partners in these long-term commercial partnerships pool their resources and skills and cooperate to accomplish their shared goals.

Strategic partnerships are collaborations in which two (or more) companies work together to accomplish their shared goals and promote growth. While maintaining their individual identities, both businesses collaborate in key areas and split any associated risks and rewards.

There is always more to this sort of partnership than merely a fleeting friendship or connection. Instead, they are enduring obligations requiring a great deal of communication, trust, and mutual effort. The idea is that the strategic partner can provide resources that the other partner finds difficult to get, such as knowledge, audience share, services, or other resources.

How do you identify and cultivate strategic partnerships that can benefit your organization's growth and success?

Strategic partnerships have much to offer, but managing them well can be difficult. Overcoming risk, managing virtual teams from many firms, deciding how to share or isolate private knowledge, and keeping open lines of communication are just a few of the challenges. In light of that, the following advice can help you create a fruitful partnership.

1. Identify the right partner.

Selecting the appropriate partner organization is always the first step. You must first be very clear about the goals you have for this partnership. McKinsey advises posing three questions to oneself:[4]

- What should the partnership achieve?
- What gaps do you need to fill?
- What opportunity do you want to capitalize on?

You may start looking for possible partners as soon as you clearly understand your partnership goals. To create a large list of possibilities, go through your current contact networks, search associations and organizations in your field, and network at conferences.

Next, review your extensive list of potential partners to see whether they have the skills you require to achieve your goals. Take into account elements such as their standing and market penetration in the small company sector, history of providing value-added services to comparable customers, and technical prowess.

---

[4] https://medium.com/lessons-from-mckinsey/the-rule-of-3-c1cd82dbc96e

To maintain alignment and reduce potential conflicts, it's critical to consider if they will fit in with your corporate culture and business principles. You should also conduct due diligence on their financial health and readiness to adjust to changing market conditions. Finally, but just as importantly, see if the other firm is open to working closely with you to handle the unique demands that small businesses have.

2. Foster communication and trust.

Like every relationship, strategic partnerships require a strong foundation of communication and trust to succeed. As business mediation and conflict resolution expert David Gage stated, "The essential elements of a successful partnership are a good fit between the partners' personalities, similar values, the ability to be a team player, compatible goals and clear expectations, and mutual trust and respect."

This starts from the very beginning of establishing a partnership. It's important to find out what benefits your prospective partner hopes to gain from the relationship. Be upfront and honest with your partner about your goals and the skills you bring to the table to set clear expectations from the start.

You need constant, honest communication to build a trusting environment. Establish easily accessible lines of communication to distribute updates and business intelligence regularly. Information sharing is facilitated by frequent meetings, assigned points of contact, and cooperative platforms.

You should also exhibit dependability by keeping your word, being accessible, and lending assistance when required. Cementing trust and developing effective communication channels requires spending time in relationship-building activities, personalizing conversations, and demonstrating a sincere dedication to your shared achievement.

3. Explore partnership models.

To select the strategic partnership that best suits your goals, you must carefully weigh the numerous possibilities. Models of strategic partners include:

- Partnership marketing, where you work together on strategic marketing campaigns.
- Distribution or reseller partnerships, where you share each other's distribution channels.
- Product partnerships or technology partnerships, where you link both your capabilities and features to produce new products or improve existing ones.
- Joint ventures, where you share both the risks and rewards of the collaboration.

The ideal partnership depends on several factors, including shared goals, available resources, and the intended degree of cooperation. A strategic partnership approach that prioritizes assistance, knowledge-sharing, and resource-sharing may prove advantageous for big firms that cater to small enterprises.

Your strategic partnership model will need to be adjusted to provide for simplicity of deployment, scalability, and flexibility. By doing this, you'll be able to make use of the bigger organization's capabilities while ensuring alignment with the particular dynamics of supporting small enterprises. Lastly, keep in mind that the partnership model will need to be periodically assessed and modified in light of changing needs.

4. Handle dispute settlement and risk management.

Conflicts between strategic partners can occur even with excellent communication and a high degree of trust. Risk management should always be proactive. Establish proactive planning and risk mitigation strategies by conducting collaborative risk assessments that thoroughly evaluate possible risks, including financial, operational, and reputational risks.

Establishing roles, duties, and expectations clearly from the outset will help reduce the likelihood of misunderstandings and confrontations. Another smart idea is to set a clear procedure for conflict resolution. The establishment of a unique collaborative unit also enables and supports strategic partnerships.

To ensure that risk management strategies and dispute resolution processes are still appropriate and useful for your partnership, regularly review and adjust them. Above all, stress the value of reaching agreements and working toward win-win solutions. Promote candid communication and active listening. Skillfully navigating disagreements and keeping the partnership's broad objectives front and center makes maintaining the health and durability of the partnership possible.

5. Continuously assess success.

Establishing measures to gauge progress and success is critical since a strategic partnership is, by definition, a long-term engagement. Setting KPIs in line with your goals is the first step.

Select quantitative and qualitative measures, such as increase in revenue, acquisition of new customers, market expansion, customer happiness, and the development of novel services or solutions specifically for small companies. To evaluate the partnership's overall performance, consider other factors such as the effectiveness of resource use, the degree of collaboration within the partnership, and the accomplishment of predetermined milestones.

Arrange periodic assessments of these KPIs to monitor advancement and pinpoint opportunities for enhancement. Having feedback sessions with small company clients is a smart way to learn how satisfied they are and generate ideas.

Have regular meetings with your strategic partner's representatives to obtain useful insights and enhance your understanding of their changing demands. A flexible approach to KPIs and evaluation techniques will guarantee their applicability and reactivity to shifting market conditions, enabling long-term success and ongoing development.

Final Thoughts - Chapter 14

Identifying and cultivating strategic partnerships is a nuanced process that requires clarity, communication, and continuous evaluation. Begin by identifying the right partner, considering what the partnership should achieve, which gaps it should fill, and what opportunities it can help capitalize on. Foster open communication and build trust to ensure a strong foundation. Explore different partnership models to find the best fit, and establish mechanisms for dispute settlement and risk management to navigate challenges effectively. Continuously assess the partnership's success to ensure it remains aligned with your organization's growth and goals. Without these deliberate efforts, partnerships can falter, leading to missed opportunities and potential setbacks. By thoughtfully selecting and nurturing these alliances, you can unlock new avenues for innovation, drive sustainable growth, and achieve remarkable success together.

JOURNAL

How do you identify and cultivate strategic partnerships that can benefit your organization's growth and success?

_____

_____

_____

_____

_____

_____

_____

_____

_____

_____

_____

_____

_____

_____

15

CRISIS MANAGEMENT

"Never waste a good crisis."
–Winston Churchill, Former Prime Minister of the United Kingdom

I n a crisis, effective leaders are the calm in the eye of the storm. Every team, company, or organization will eventually face a crisis or unanticipated emergency, whether they like it or not. In rapidly evolving businesses, most teams and leaders face a crisis of some kind almost every week, and in certain situations, it seems like they happen every day. Even if these circumstances are not nearly as serious as a catastrophic earthquake, tsunami, or worldwide epidemic, they may still cause chaos for a company and make team members anxious and stressed.

Anticipating and preparing for crises in advance is the most effective approach to handling them. Proactive thinking and planning help people be better equipped to handle any unpleasant situations that may arise.

However, certain occurrences will be so hard to predict that they will catch almost everyone off guard, even with the finest scenario planning and preparedness.

Having worked in politics for so many years, I have had my fair share of exposure to scandals. In senior roles, I have helped to manage the fallout of those scandals and manage staff while also battling my health issues. The magnitude of one scandal was so great that it dragged on for two years, scarring the careers of many staff members (including my own). It resulted in having to obtain a white-collar criminal defense attorney for federal grand jury testimony, all while also receiving a cancer diagnosis. As I reflect back on this experience, my first thought is, *WTF... No one would ever believe this!* But it's true. That really happened. And I navigated the situation with grace, emotional agility, and quiet confidence. My team members and I did not realize it at the time, but we did a lot of things right. The tactics and strategies I mention here were executed for the most part, and I am very proud of that. Our diversity of collective talents and experiences came together to manage a very tumultuous situation.

Successful leaders are aware that managing crises is not novel. Since the beginning of civilization, crises have existed, and they will continue to occur. Great leaders rise to the challenge despite the fact that chaos may be complicated, disruptive, and cause fear inside the firm. Less successful leaders tend to act in a panic, think illogically, and make bad choices.

If you're in command during a crisis, make sure you lead in a way that keeps perspective, adaptability, and presence in mind.

Most leaders are obliged to think and act in unusual ways during a crisis. They must adopt an emergency response strategy and adapt it when new information and circumstances arise, whether it be a technical, financial, environmental, or health crisis at work or in the community.

Effective leaders are able to maintain their composure and perspective throughout. "During a crisis, your job is to limit loss and keep things working as normal as possible," says Gene Klann, author of the book *Crisis Leadership.*[5]

---

[5] https://www.linkedin.com/pulse/how-lead-through-crisis-adrienne-lawler?trk=portfolio_article-card_title

How do you effectively lead and manage your team during times of crisis or emergency?

So, what happens when crises arise quickly and violently? Regardless of the magnitude or time of any crisis or emergency, there are a few crucial actions you can take to control the crisis and lessen the harm it may inflict on you and your company. Here is a methodical and useful structure to help you and your team navigate unknown territory:

1. Consider the situation before acting.

When a crisis arises, the first thing you need to do is remain composed. Leaders must exercise some self-control to prevent being immobilized. Your mind needs time to take in the events of a crisis before you can take charge of the situation. It will be more challenging to perceive the issue clearly through the chaos if you don't take things slowly. Gaining the upper hand may become difficult as a result.

When the sky seems to be falling, pause, take a deep breath, and make an effort to reason through the circumstances. It can feel strange to wait and consider your answer carefully since your primal inclination urges you to freeze, panic, and then go in different directions, but it's critical that you do so.

Ensure that your team knows they can count on you. Maintaining composure and engaging in self-coaching will soothe your team.

An inner conversation is necessary to summon mental control. "This isn't the first time something like this has occurred," "You can do this," "You will survive this," or "Slow down and properly examine the issue" are some examples of self-coaching phrases. Finding your calm voice in the midst of the pandemonium is crucial.

Another method for managing your thoughts when you are in unfamiliar territory is to get in touch with a trusted colleague who has worked with you in the past and who isn't involved in the crisis. They will be able to provide you with some unbiased advice and help you adopt a fresh viewpoint on the matter.

2. Describe the crisis to your team.

The definition of the crisis is the next "must-do." In other words, put together a succinct and straightforward declaration or explanation of the crisis you're in. The way you break the news to your team members may have a big impact on how they respond.

Explaining the circumstances logically reassures people that the crisis can be resolved. Use a brief problem description that consists of the following before communicating the message to your team:

- Who is involved?
- What is affected?
- Where is it happening?
- When did you first become aware of it?

3. What to do when defining a crisis.

Make it clear what is and is not happening in the circumstance. For instance, do you mean the entire facility or simply the production and shipping areas when you say there is a "power outage at the factory?"

Include pertinent facts to maintain perspective. Many times, the initial phases of a crisis are overstated. It's important not to downplay your current situation; you want a truthful and realistic account of what has happened or is happening.

Have patience. Determining the shape, look, or structure of the crisis may seem difficult at first. However, as you describe the problem and create a picture, you will be in a better position to enlist help and decide on a course of action.

4. What not to do when defining a crisis.

Avoid getting bogged down in a comprehensive diagnostic examination or analysis. You are only attempting to make sense of the limits of your situation and the effects of this tragic turn of events.

Above all, avoid blaming or pointing fingers. This will not make much of a difference in your triage attempts.

5. Establish priorities.

Leaders must prioritize the problems and challenges they are experiencing because focused efficiency is essential during a crisis. Leaders who are able to persevere in the face of turmoil and challenges recognize that no two crises are the same in terms of their extent or breadth and that dealing with many crises at once is common.

Quiet is necessary for setting priorities and figuring out what is essential, time-sensitive, and changing in scope and size. Setting priorities involves more than just providing a brief, high-level explanation or summary. You also need to collect unbiased data and facts about the crisis's gravity, immediacy, and growth.

6. Assess the seriousness.

Accurately assessing the event's seriousness is a prerequisite for starting the recovery process after a crisis. This entails assessing the situation's possible effect, scope, and seriousness. Consider whether the crisis is a less serious one or a mission-critical one (an existential danger). A normal customer complaint on a small issue is not the same as a mission-critical crisis.

Remember, many people want your crisis to be theirs. You need to know when to go into crisis mode yourself, when to respond appropriately, and when to be willing to help other team members through their own crises.

7. Determine the urgency.

You must determine the urgency of dealing with the issue after determining its importance. This means calculating the rate of change and the amount of time you have left to stop the bleeding and reduce your losses. You must determine if you are dealing with a gradual, manageable burn or a rapidly spreading wildfire. A large, rapidly spreading fire will demand a quicker and more thorough reaction than a threat that is approaching more slowly.

8. Factor the potential growth.

Consider the crisis's potential growth or spread. This can be achieved by determining whether the crisis is manageable and unlikely to worsen or spread or whether it will lead to other issues. If the crisis is not becoming worse or if the trend line is flat or dropping, you have some time and space to come up with a solution.

9. Determine solutions for handling the crisis with your team.

Once the problem's priority has been established, you and your team may collaborate to develop your alternatives, the options available to you, and the desired results for resolving the crisis. If you can specify the intended results, you can reduce the number of possible responses to a small number. This enables you to get comfortable and concentrate on the specifics so that your plan can be implemented properly.

At this point, talk about the best course of action with your team and weigh the advantages and disadvantages of the options available to you.

Acknowledge that you are still not operating at a tactical level. That is the following item. Returning to the fire metaphor, you will need to determine whether it is preferable to tackle the fire from the air or the ground.

In certain circumstances, you may even be able to perform both, but it's often the opposite. For example, combating the fire by air might be your only recourse if you find yourself in a hilly area. Perhaps it would be best to just stand down and assess the situation later if there is a lot of rain in the forecast. Effective crisis managers are aware that sometimes they have to choose between two unpleasant alternatives, but they also know that they need to act in the best interests of the situation.

10. Create an action plan.

Now that you and your team have objectively examined the problem and determined your possibilities, you can rapidly devise a plan of action. There is never enough time to plan everything out in a crisis. In fact, you might only have time to halt the bleeding and implement a temporary, stopgap solution.

A stopgap solution is an intermediate strategy. It will give you more time to develop a more comprehensive, corrective solution to stabilize the situation, avert a crisis in the future, or organize backup plans to lessen the effects of disasters.

In this stage, you allocate and deploy resources, create a strategy, assign responsibilities to team members, and rank your activities according to the priority or difficulty of the issues you are trying to solve. The secret is to prioritize your tasks so that, given the time available, you can get the best results.

11. Come together to act on the plan.

After implementing a strategy, it's time to start making progress and gathering momentum to address the crisis. Make sure you have a few basic indicators set up so you can tell what is and isn't working. Allocate your time, effort, and resources to the tasks that are most crucial and will alleviate the immediate strain and anxiety on your group and team.

You should anticipate some early blunders, confusion, overlaps, and redundancies while you are acting quickly. Urge your team to remain focused on the main issue and avoid becoming distracted by these little issues.

Acknowledge that overshooting and waste occur when you are in crisis management mode.

As you organize your response, make sure you provide your team with encouraging feedback when genuine progress is being made. Honor any progress made and never give up. Even when the news is bad, you still need to be honest and provide all the details.

12. Effectively deliver the message to external parties.

It is impossible to overvalue the importance of how you communicate when managing a team in crisis. Remember that rumors and false information travel quickly when you launch your attack on the crisis. A basic communication structure that specifies what information will be transmitted to immediate leaders and by whom has to be established.

You must also choose what information is shared with other teams, stakeholders in the company, peers, and coworkers. Determining the tactics to be used and the amount of information to communicate with those on the front lines is crucial. Make sure your team is included in these preparations to ensure that they are informed of the upcoming phases.

Choose your communication strategy, the pertinent information to convey, and the appropriate timing for sharing it with external stakeholders. People who are not in constant communication will usually assume the worst. Be prepared to face hard truths and refrain from downplaying the challenges you are encountering. Evaluating your audience's demands will help you portray these challenges accurately. Remember that the procedure involves extensive repetition, so be ready to say the same thing several times in various ways.

Since every crisis is unique, a unique solution is needed. It is easy to go overboard with any of the "must-do" tasks. Please try to respond as succinctly, simply, and efficiently as possible without excluding any crucial information. Effective crisis managers are usually everlasting optimists. Just make sure that your optimism doesn't make you seem out of touch with reality. Even among your fans, your reputation can suffer if you are too hopeful.

Leaders take the high road and hope for the best but are always ready for challenging situations. To face the unknowns that come with every crisis, a leader must accept responsibility for their mental state and maintain an honest line of communication with their team. Throughout a crisis, locate your partners and supporters and stay emotionally connected to your team.

Great leaders prepare for the unexpected. They are aware that chaos can take many forms, from little disturbances to major catastrophes. Understanding that disappointments and setbacks are inevitable while leading a team during a crisis is essential. When you have knowledgeable people on your team, you can weather any storm together with ease, knowing that it will pass even though you don't always know when the next one will arrive.

Final Thoughts - Chapter 15

Act as a leader, and don't let circumstances outside your control make you or your team feel victimized. Effective leaders keep an eye out for team members who might be about to lose it and offer comfort and support. Even while they are aware that there are certain things they will never be able to alter, they never give up on helping others or giving them the confidence and skills they need to handle emergencies and return to some semblance of normalcy.

JOURNAL

How do you effectively lead and manage your team during times of crisis or emergency?

16

DECISION-MAKING UNDER PRESSURE

"In a moment of decision, the best thing you can do is the right thing to do, the next best thing is the wrong thing, and the worst thing you can do is nothing."
–Theodore Roosevelt, 26th President of the United States

T he crucible of pressure can forge the strongest decisions. Leaders must frequently make decisions while under pressure. They aren't always afforded sufficient time to consider all relevant factors before deciding on a plan of action. When this occurs, leaders must act swiftly and forcefully.

How do you maintain a clear and rational decision-making process when under pressure?

Making decisions under duress may be dangerous, difficult, and unpleasant. You have to move quickly and decisively whether you are dealing with an urgent emergency, a high-stakes scenario, or an unanticipated disaster. How can you prevent errors, pass up chances, or compromise your morals? How do you make expert decisions under duress?

1. Clear your mind.

Calm down to make sense of things. Critical decisions that affect businesses, staff, and consumers are usually made under pressure.

Approaching the situation with clarity can reduce needless risk and help you make the best decisions. Picture the results and then give yourself some time to contemplate.

2. Determine the desired outcome.

Recognize the circumstances and reach a consensus on the intended result. Next, take advantage of the time you have to examine the activities, dangers, and success factors. Sometimes, a choice may be divided into manageable phases, allowing you to choose the first one while you continue to hone your overall plan. Keep an eye on developments and have backup plans in case things start to go off course. Adaptability is essential.

3. Put crucial elements first.

Making decisions involves weighing a variety of elements, including the availability and quality of your data, the decision's potential effects on your organization, your prior experience making similar decisions, your available options, and the cost of delaying the decision. A competent decision-maker weighs the variables in real-time, giving priority to those that are significant, intricate, and time-sensitive.

4. Make intuitive decisions.

When it comes to making decisions, following your gut feeling is the best course of action when you are pressed for time. Merriam-Webster defines intuition as "the ability or faculty of acquiring immediate knowledge or cognition without obvious rational deliberation and inference."[6] The development of intuition comes from experience and time. Being able to use that is essential for a leader.

---

[6] https://www.merriam-webster.com/

5. Be ready for any possible repercussions.

As decision-makers, leaders are unable to predict how their choices will turn out. But when leaders are forced to make a snap decision, they should thoroughly weigh all of their options and the possible outcomes of each. If one option seems like the best one at the time, leaders should take the appropriate action and get ready for any fallout.

6. Consider desirability and probability when making decisions.

Desirability and likelihood must be considered when making any decision. As a corporate leader, it is your responsibility to make the best outcome the most likely. To do this, run scenarios on each choice. After projecting the outcome of your choice, balance the potential risks and benefits. Select the course of action that minimizes total risk while meeting the criteria of attractiveness and likelihood.

7. Understand the issue.

Rethink the way you make decisions. Different decisions call for different amounts of thought and preparation. Make an effort to comprehend the issue or subproblem you are attempting to resolve, as well as its advantages and potential repercussions. Examining the data you currently have and the actions you must take to make a choice are equally important. These responses can steer you away from overanalyzing and encourage you to make better decisions more quickly.

8. Use decision matrices.

Decision matrices are useful for placing ideas in context, particularly when there is limited time. Consider using a straightforward four-square, where the X-axis represents Reversible/Irreversible and the Y-axis represents Inconsequential/Consequential. The only quadrant you should be concerned about making mistakes in when under time constraints is the upper-right quadrant (Consequential/Irreversible). You can assign or convert the rest into a brief, direct message.

9. Consider the timing and the need for additional data.

My preferred method for making important decisions is to apply Jeff Bezos's well-known 70% rule:[7] use 70% of the knowledge you wish you had to make decisions. Yes, it's not all worked out, but who will figure it out if you do not? Consider the importance of accuracy versus sufficient facts to make quick decisions. If you wait for further details, you could sometimes be late and end up losing. You will ultimately need to adjust and alter, of course, but start now.

10. Divide issues into their most basic components.

To ascertain the exact mix of significance and reversibility you are dealing with, apply the first principles technique. An assumption that cannot be further inferred is called a first principle. The idea is to disassemble complicated issues into their most fundamental components and then piece them back together. This can help you choose the optimal course of action by distilling the choice down to the essentials.

11. Brainstorm benefits and drawbacks.

As much as you can, deliberately look for both positive and negative aspects. We frequently—and sometimes unconsciously—seek choices or information that support our own opinions. Understanding this is crucial since doing so will help you handle the transition process more skillfully.

---

[7] https://www.linkedin.com/pulse/making-better-business-decisions-jeff-bezos-70-rule-zegarelli

12. Acknowledge and consider your assumptions.

No matter when a choice is made, be sure you know what you're assuming, how probable it is that these assumptions are true, and what will probably happen if one or more of them are false. It's a safe move if you can tolerate the possibility of being wrong and you are really certain that your assumptions are accurate.

Final Thoughts - Chapter 16

It is vital to recognize that the ability to make sound decisions in the heat of the moment is one of the most defining traits of effective leadership. The crucible of pressure doesn't just test your decision-making skills—it refines them, turning challenges into opportunities for growth and resilience. In these moments, when time is scarce, and the stakes are high, your ability to remain clear-headed, focused, and decisive will set you apart as a leader.

The strategies outlined here provide a framework for navigating these intense situations with confidence and clarity. From clearing your mind to prioritize critical elements, to trusting your intuition and using decision matrices to organize your thoughts, each approach equips you to handle pressure with poise. The ability to swiftly analyze, act, and adapt under pressure is what transforms a leader from good to great.

Remember, decision-making under pressure is not about perfection; it's about making the best possible choices with the information and time available to you. By embracing these techniques, you can reduce risks, capitalize on opportunities, and maintain your ethical standards, even in the most challenging circumstances. As you refine these skills, you'll not only improve your own decision-making but also inspire confidence and trust within your team, driving your organization toward sustained success.

JOURNAL

How do you maintain a clear and rational decision-making process when under pressure?

_____

_____

_____

_____

_____

_____

_____

_____

_____

_____

_____

_____

_____

17

EMOTIONAL INTELLIGENCE

"Leadership is not domination, but the art of persuading
people to work toward a common goal."
–Daniel Goleman, Author *of Emotional Intelligence*

E mbrace the power of empathy and self-awareness.
An industry as fast-paced as software development needs emotionally intelligent leaders since no one performs at their best when they don't feel understood or cared for.

The capacity to control your emotions and those of the people around you is referred to as emotional intelligence or EQ. People with high emotional intelligence are able to interpret their feelings, understand the significance of those feelings for themselves, and understand how their actions impact people around them.

High emotional intelligence is a crucial component of being a good leader. It has five essential components: self-awareness, self-regulation, motivation, empathy, and social skills. Your level of emotional intelligence increases with how well you can handle each of these crucial areas.

Let's examine each of these components in more detail:

Self-Awareness

Being self-aware means being aware of your feelings at all times and understanding how your behavior might influence other people. Knowing your advantages and disadvantages as a leader gives you more control over your behavior.

Jotting down your ideas can increase your self-awareness. Regulating your response during intense emotional moments can also enhance it.

Self-Regulation

Maintaining emotional control is the foundation of self-regulation. Effective leaders hardly ever misuse their power, become angry with their staff when things get tough, or make snap judgments.

Understanding your values can help you become more adept at self-regulation, which will make it simpler for you to make moral or ethical decisions. Another way to self-regulate is to take responsibility for your actions rather than blaming others when anything goes wrong.

Motivation

Self-motivated leaders set high standards for themselves, work steadily toward their objectives, and never stop inspiring their team members. They move on without being compulsive because they have a positive emotional bond with the outcome they want to achieve. Reminding yourself of the aspects of your work that you enjoy can help you become more motivated. It also helps you maintain optimism and see the positive side of any difficult circumstance.

Empathy

The capacity to imagine oneself in another person's shoes is known as empathy. Empathy is a crucial quality of effective leaders. Being empathetic means supporting the growth of your team members, checking on unhappy individuals, providing constructive criticism to those who need it, and listening to those who need to vent.

By constantly putting yourself in other people's shoes and considering situations from their perspective, you can increase your empathy. Observing body language closely may also help you increase your empathy as it helps you understand what the other person is thinking and respond accordingly.

Be aware of your emotions and act accordingly. Rather than brushing off an employee's unhappiness when you ask them to accomplish anything, address their concerns and show them that you are aware of them.

Social Skills

Effective communicators with strong emotional intelligence are leaders in success. They are adept at managing both positive and negative news, inspiring their team to support them, and igniting enthusiasm for new endeavors. They are skilled at mediating disputes amicably.

They also do an excellent job of leading by example. By developing your communication abilities, understanding how to resolve conflicts, and learning how to compliment people, you may enhance and expand your social skills.

Effective leaders are the foundation of every company. A lack of emotional intelligence may lead to a decrease in employee engagement, which might have more serious repercussions.

Being an excellent worker is not enough to make you a great leader; without the ability to communicate with your team effectively, your results will be subpar. You need to be emotionally intelligent to progress in your career and organization.

How do you use emotional intelligence to navigate challenging situations and build strong relationships with your team?

Now, let's break this down into smaller questions so you can get the hang of it easily.

Your life and leadership will change if you take the time to thoughtfully and honestly respond to these questions.

Strong leaders with high emotional intelligence pose the following seven questions to themselves on a regular basis:

1. Is the goal consistent and clearly stated?

A capable leader establishes a distinct and coherent vision for the business or group. A leader must ensure that everyone is aware of the company's values, mission, and business goals. A leader must also illustrate how each individual contributes to the final result.

An emotionally intelligent leader provides information in a timely and open manner. They communicate updates and share developments on the team's or company's progress toward realizing the goal. Emotionally intelligent leaders understand that constant communication is necessary to build trust and loyalty because it keeps everyone on the same page about their objectives.

2. Does my team feel capable?

Emotionally intelligent leaders must tread lightly. When things start to get out of control, they provide their followers the autonomy to take over and complete their tasks. They are aware that their role is to maintain the company's and the team's focus on having the most positive effect possible.

A strong leader gives their people the freedom to make wise decisions, learn from their errors, and have the room they need to accomplish their duties properly. When anything goes wrong, emotionally intelligent leaders know when to intervene and give their team space.

3. Is there a sense of purpose among my team members?

Emotionally intelligent leaders understand that their team must be motivated and feel that their work matters every day. Leaders are aware of the necessity of giving their team a sense of direction, and they are aware that it makes sense.

Effective leaders ensure that their team members perceive themselves as valuable contributors, feel included in decision-making, and contribute to the company's expansion. Emotionally intelligent leaders understand that their team members will go above and beyond if they are given a purpose.

4. Is it fun for my team to come to work?

Emotionally intelligent leaders inspire and motivate their teams to perform at their highest level. They are aware that their crew has to look forward to going to work every day. They glance in the mirror because they understand that they have to set an example for others. Are they excited to go to work? If so, their team will be, too.

Strong leaders understand that for their team to enjoy their work, they must be encouraged and given constructive criticism. They are aware that they must make room and pave the way for the team. Cheerleaders and coaches are examples of emotionally intelligent leaders. They put themselves in their team's position and demonstrate empathy.

5. How well do I listen?

Strong emotional intelligence makes a leader a skilled communicator. Such leaders pay excellent attention. They are aware that effective communication starts with listening, but they also know that hearing is only one aspect of the process.

Effective leaders understand that listening is the first step in effectively communicating their message and ideas. They can handle small problems before they become major ones since they are aware of what is going on with their team. They understand that listening is just as important as speaking.

6. Does the group believe it can accomplish its objectives?

Emotionally intelligent leaders know each team member's objectives and are aware of the kinds of professions they seek. They frequently inquire about their group's satisfaction with their work. Strong leaders also inquire about their professional development during one-on-one sessions.

Effective leaders understand that for their team to accomplish goals, certain "red tape" and bureaucracy must be removed. Asking their team whether they can accomplish their objectives and, if not, what they can do to make them happen is a strong sign of an emotionally intelligent leader.

7. Are team members' efforts acknowledged when they exceed expectations?

High emotional intelligence leaders are always looking for opportunities to express gratitude to their team members. They honor exceptional accomplishments and efforts that influence the business and other divisions.

Effective leaders are aware that expressing gratitude to certain people works best. They are aware that their staff will get resentful and cease to go above and beyond if their outstanding work is not acknowledged. Emotionally intelligent leaders take the time to get to know their team members and recognize their contributions.

Once you're able to answer these questions, you're good to go.

Final Thoughts - Chapter 17

As you reflect on the vital role emotional intelligence plays in your leadership journey, remember that it's more than just a skill—it's a way of being that transforms how you lead, connect, and inspire others. Over the years, I've passionately preached the importance of emotional intelligence to colleagues and friends alike, knowing that its impact on leadership is profound. The ability to be self-aware, to regulate emotions, to stay motivated, and to genuinely empathize with others forms the foundation of not just good leadership, but extraordinary leadership. By regularly asking yourself the seven key questions outlined in this chapter, you'll foster a work environment where your team feels valued, motivated, and capable of achieving great things.

As an executive coach and a devoted practitioner of emotional intelligence, I can attest that mastering these principles will not only elevate your leadership but also deepen the trust and respect you cultivate within your team. This is the true power of emotional intelligence—transforming challenges into opportunities and building a legacy of leadership that endures.

JOURNAL

How do you use emotional intelligence to navigate challenging situations and build strong relationships with your team?

_____

_____

_____

_____

_____

_____

_____

_____

_____

_____

_____

_____

_____

_____

_____

18

TEAM BUILDING

"Talent wins games, but teamwork and intelligence win championships."
–Michael Jordan, Six-time NBA Champion

T eamwork is the collaborative engine of success. Consider how you can foster a culture of cooperation and friendship.

Have you ever been a part of a group that seemed to "click?" The sort where you do amazing things with ease, and everyone appears to understand one another without exchanging words? That's the allure of team synergy, which transforms the landscape of cooperation.

As entrepreneurs, we recognize the value of teamwork in the workplace, but we also acknowledge the challenges that result from fusing unique skills and personalities.

Collaboration and communication are fostered by teamwork, which facilitates employees' ability to manage their workload. It serves as a company's binding agent.

How do you foster collaboration, cohesion, and synergy within your team?

Collaboration and cohesion within a team are crucial for its success. In a harmonious team environment, members exchange ideas, skills, and viewpoints to solve issues in novel and efficient ways.

Let's discuss how to build team cohesion and cooperation inside your organization, resulting in a productive and happy work environment.

1. Use efficient techniques and resources.

Optimizing cooperation with your team requires that you set up a clear, well-organized working process. Select the appropriate resources to help with task completion and communication.

2. Promote honest and transparent communication.

Effective communication is essential for any successful team effort. Members of the team should be encouraged to ask questions, share ideas, and express themselves openly. Establish a setting where everyone may participate without feeling judged or uncomfortable. To encourage idea sharing and cooperation, schedule frequent team meetings with a specific goal in mind, conduct brainstorming sessions, and set up discussion threads.

3. Establish a shared objective and set of values.

The team is united by a single vision created by a defined goal and shared values. When creating goals, include everyone on your team and make sure they all know how their efforts fit into the bigger picture. A shared objective improves team cohesion by fostering a sense of companionship, belonging, and shared accountability. Stress the importance of team values like mutual support, trust, and respect and exhort everyone to live up to them in their everyday interactions.

4. Foster diverse and complementary skills.

People with different but complementary skills work well together on a high-performing team. To ensure that each team member can contribute differently, promote diversity in hiring and training. Combining different skills fosters problem-solving, innovation, and group decision-making.

5. Plan activities to promote teamwork and strengthen cohesion.

Plan frequent team-building exercises outside of the office. These enjoyable and cooperative exercises can deepen team members' camaraderie, forge personal bonds, and help them get to know one another better. Games, seminars, team-building exercises, and volunteer work are a few examples of activities that can strengthen team cohesion. To prevent counter-productiveness, specify a clear goal to be accomplished at the conclusion of these activities.

6. Celebrate collective achievements.

Make time to recognize and honor noteworthy achievements with team outings, gifts, or words of gratitude. Maintaining motivation and cohesion requires praising each team member's contributions and accomplishments. Congratulate team members publicly for their accomplishments, both individually and as a group, and express gratitude for their commitment and hard work. Acknowledgment creates a happy atmosphere and motivates further cooperation.

Final Thoughts - Chapter 18

Building team cohesion and collaboration is a continuous effort that requires dedication from management and every team member. You can build a work atmosphere where cooperation thrives and each team member can thrive by promoting open communication, creating a common objective and shared values, supporting diversity and inclusion, encouraging teamwork and delegating, and recognizing collective successes.

Collaboration and cohesion foster innovation, improve team performance, and aid in the accomplishment of shared objectives. By putting money into these techniques, you can create a cohesive, effective team that succeeds at what it does.

JOURNAL

How do you foster collaboration, cohesion, and synergy within your team?

19

BUILDING HIGH-PERFORMING TEAMS

High-performing teams are the engines of achievement.
"None of us is as smart as all of us."
–Ken Blanchard, Author of *Leading at a Higher Level*

Why are some teams better than others? What distinguishes these teams from the others? How can you build exceptional teams?

There are several reasons why teams perform differently. While each team is different, high-performing teams have a few things in common.

Throughout my career, I've had the honor of establishing and leading outstanding teams in various capacities. I have personally observed the intriguing dynamics that set high-performing teams apart from the competition.

How do you create an environment where team members are empowered to excel and achieve their full potential?

Building a high-performing workforce is crucial to your organization's success. Amazing things happen when people work together, motivated by a common goal and armed with the appropriate strategies.

These useful tips can help you create a cooperative and high-performing work environment, whether you are a business leader, manager, or team member.

1. Establish a clear goal and vision.

The foundation of any high-performing team is a clear goal and vision. Establish the team's objectives, goals, and shared vision for success. As this will be the team's compass during their cooperation, make sure each member is aware of and supportive of the vision.

Fostering open communication, active listening, and respect for other viewpoints is essential to building a high-performing team. Establish official and informal lines of communication to ensure everyone is informed, involved, and able to voice their opinions.

2. Promote psychological safety and trust.

High-performing teams are built on a foundation of trust. Create a trusting atmosphere where team members feel able to take risks, express their thoughts, and err without worrying about being judged. Promote cooperation, openness, and respect for one another to strengthen team relationships.

3. Accept diversity and inclusion.

Diverse teams provide a multitude of viewpoints, concepts, and experiences. To promote diversity and inclusivity, ensure that team members have a variety of experiences, skill sets, and perspectives. Foster a welcoming atmosphere that values individual uniqueness and encourages cooperation.

4. Clearly define roles and responsibilities.

Well-defined positions and duties promote responsibility and structure. Assign work in accordance with each person's interests, skills, and talents. Make sure everyone is aware of their responsibilities and how they fit into the larger picture of the team's performance. To maximize effectiveness, evaluate positions often and realign them as necessary.

5. Encourage learning and development.

Promote continuous learning and development. Offer mentoring, training, and professional development opportunities. Create a supportive atmosphere to encourage team members to exchange information, grow their abilities, and remain up to speed on best practices and industry developments.

6. Promote teamwork and cooperation.

High-performing teams are built on synergy and cooperation. Encourage a cooperative atmosphere where team members build on and enhance each other's abilities. Facilitate brainstorming sessions, cross-functional teamwork, and a shared feeling of responsibility to accomplish group goals.

7. Honor accomplishments and acknowledge contributions.

Gratitude and acknowledgment are strong inducements to work harder and better. Honor individual efforts, group accomplishments, and significant anniversaries. Recognize a job well done and provide constructive feedback. This promotes sustained high performance and strengthens the team culture.

Final Thoughts - Chapter 19

Building a high-performing team requires a combination of strategic planning, effective communication, trust, diversity, and continuous development. Implementing these strategies can establish a dynamic and cooperative work environment where your team accomplishes exceptional outcomes and propels your organization forward. Realize your organization's potential by embracing the strength of a high-performing team.

JOURNAL

How do you create an environment where team members are empowered to excel and achieve their full potential?

_____

_____

_____

_____

_____

_____

_____

_____

_____

_____

_____

_____

_____

_____

20

LEADING REMOTE TEAMS

*"Leadership is about making others better as a result of your presence
and making sure that impact lasts in your absence."*
–Sheryl Sandberg, Author of *Lean In*

D istance leadership requires a unique touch. In March 2020, neither employers nor workers predicted the rapid shift to remote work from home. Unsurprisingly, a Harvard poll conducted early in the COVID-19 epidemic revealed that 41% of leaders found it difficult to maintain the engagement of their remote team members, and 40% of leaders were ill-prepared to manage remote workers. Similarly, just 40% of workers who did their job from home said they felt their supervisors supported them.[8]

Remote employment is here to stay. Many managers are uncertain about the most effective ways to complete tasks because they are burdened with managing the performance of team members who are more distributed, working from home, in the office, and in various time zones. As expected, many managers would rather have their employees come back to work, but when they propose this, they encounter opposition and even outright disobedience.

---

[8] https://hbr.org/2022/10/what-great-remote-managers-do-differently

A remote manager has to set up efficient technology, communication, and processes for their remote staff, just like they would with an in-person team. Although managing teams that you do not encounter in person every day has its quirks, many characteristics shared by onsite and colocated managers also apply to remote team managers.

How do you effectively lead and manage remote teams, ensuring productivity, engagement, and collaboration?

Due to the recent increase in remote employment, leaders now face a distinctive mix of possibilities and challenges. Although working remotely might save costs and provide flexibility, it requires a different leadership style. For remote workers to remain motivated and productive, it is critical to prioritize excellent communication, cooperation, and trust.

We'll examine five strategies for leading remote teams to success. These strategies include building relationships virtually, emphasizing autonomy and trust, and encouraging communication and teamwork.

1. Encourage interaction and teamwork.

Effective teamwork and communication are critical for success when leading remote teams. Establishing norms and procedures for efficient communication, such as frequent check-ins, group meetings, and virtual collaboration tools, is also crucial. To promote a feeling of community among team members, it is important to provide chances for social contact and to encourage team members to be proactive in sharing information and ideas. Tools like Monday.com, Asana, Trello, and Slack promote teamwork and communication and keep everyone in the loop.

Regular meetings give everyone the chance to check in, talk about their status, and offer input. Additionally, they foster healthy dialogue and maintain open lines of trust. While it's a good idea to schedule these meetings regularly and to promote involvement from all team members, don't forget to create chances for social contact to help fight isolation and fortify the sense of community. This might involve online team-building exercises, informal coffee breaks, or other inventive interaction methods.

Regular one-on-one sessions, in addition to team meetings, may foster open communication and trust. At these sessions, individual team members have the chance to voice any issues or worries they may have and provide their leader feedback. Making these one-on-one meetings a priority will help you ensure your direct reports are understood and encouraged.

2. Set specific objectives and expectations.

When managing a remote team, having clear expectations and goals makes all the difference. It's critical to ensure every staff member is aware of their specific duties and obligations. This makes it more likely that everyone is working toward the same goals and able to track their progress efficiently.

Establishing individual and team goals to suitably build robust indicators for success is a fruitful approach to clearly defining expectations and goals. Give your team room to grow by letting them help create metrics and giving them a chance to prove to you that they understand the demands of the business and what is expected of them. Employees benefit from knowing what is expected of them and what they must accomplish to help the organization reach its goals. Team members can also benefit from frequent coaching and feedback to stay on task and make necessary corrections.

Project management software can facilitate assigning assignments and monitoring development in real-time. This fosters a culture where workers can change course or continue independently by giving them the ability to monitor their progress on their own schedule. It's critical for leaders to select the tool that best suits their goals and those of their business and to make sure that everyone is proficient in its use. Selecting a tool that will be used by everybody is best done by taking communication styles and company goals into consideration.

As was already said, good communication and teamwork are just as essential as project management tools. To promote a feeling of belonging and community, encourage team members to be proactive in sharing ideas and updates and create chances for social engagement. This facilitates the development of trust between leaders and individual contributors as well as between team members and business partners.

3. Prioritize autonomy and trust.

Since team members operate autonomously when working remotely, leaders must have a greater degree of trust. Leaders need to adopt a practice of clearly outlining expectations and rules, but they also need to let team members take responsibility for their work and make decisions on their own. This fosters trust and gives team members the freedom to think critically and solve problems, leading to increased engagement and work satisfaction.

To help your members develop trust and autonomy, encourage them to record their procedures and impart information to others. A common knowledge base may be established so that team members can readily access and learn from one another's experiences using tools like Notion, Confluence, SharePoint, and occasionally your company's learning management system (LMS) or customer relationship manager (CRM). By doing this, you are encouraging a culture of information sharing and continuous development.

You may also provide your team members with more resources and assistance to finish their tasks to further promote trust and autonomy. Giving them access to software, online courses, and other resources that can improve their productivity can be empowering. Maintaining constant communication with your team members is crucial to offer constructive criticism of their performance. This creates accountability and ownership while also fostering trust.

Allowing mistakes to be made so that they may be learned from is another way to empower team members to accept responsibility for their job.

In group or one-on-one meetings, as a leader, you should offer direction and support, but in the end, it is up to your team members to figure out the best answers. Encouraging originality and creativity may result in fresh ideas and innovation, which can have a big impact on your company.

4. Make work-life balance a priority.

Setting a high priority on work-life balance helps remote teams be productive and healthy. Establishing limits and encouraging staff to take breaks are important ways for leaders to support a good work-life balance. Offering tools and resources for mental health and wellbeing, such as flexible work hours and employee assistance programs, may also help staff successfully manage their work-life balance.

In a similar vein, team members may find it easier to overwork when working remotely, as it can be difficult to draw boundaries between work and personal life. Establish precise guidelines for working hours and motivate your team to take time off as needed. This guarantees that they are able to recuperate and return to work with fresh vitality and concentration, in addition to aiding in the maintenance of their well-being.

Another strategy to emphasize work-life balance is encouraging everyone to document their work procedures so they can simply pick up where they left off when they return to work. This helps staff members manage their workload and guarantees that their absence won't have a detrimental effect on the group's output. When using project management software, this strategy may be quite beneficial as it enables other team members to monitor progress and provide assistance to others as required.

Asking your staff for suggestions on how to improve balance in their lives can inspire innovative solutions that benefit all parties. Establishing limits, offering resources, and fostering an environment that values healthy breaks can support your team members in maintaining their well-being, creativity, and productivity.

5. Use data and technology.

Various tools and platforms make it possible to manage projects, track progress, and get immediate feedback. Data analysis on team involvement and performance may also point out areas for development and enable necessary changes to strategies. By embracing technology and data, leaders can make wise decisions to enhance team performance.

Analyzing data on engagement and performance helps leaders understand a team's strengths and shortcomings. This information can also help leaders enhance procedures and boost engagement by better understanding the difficulties their workers experience. Metrics such as work completion rates, communication frequency, and productivity can be tracked to identify areas that require improvement.

Using data and technology to your advantage is essential to running a remote workforce efficiently. Leaders can enhance team results by using the appropriate tools and reviewing team performance data. Project management tools, data analysis, and video conferencing platforms like Zoom or Microsoft Teams all support remote teams' productivity, organization, and communication.

To maintain stated goals and expectations, don't forget to include these insights in your group and one-on-one sessions. Though many of the above-listed project management programs include choices for producing visually striking reports on data, you can always rely on tools like Excel to generate your own original data representations, complete with charts and graphs for quick and simple comprehension.

Final Thoughts - Chapter 20

Managing remote workers is an interesting journey filled with challenges. When great distances separate you, how can you foster a feeling of belonging and camaraderie among your team? How can the flexibility and liberty that come with working remotely be balanced with the necessity for structure and direction? How can you be certain that the members of your team are managing their own well-being and striking a good work-life balance? As they traverse this brave new world, leaders of remote teams need to think about all of these questions.

You can guide yourself, your company, and your team members to success by putting a high priority on communication, cooperation, trust, and work-life balance. You can also use technology and data to inform decision-making.

JOURNAL

How do you effectively lead and manage remote teams, ensuring productivity, engagement, and collaboration?

21

BUILDING RESILIENCE IN YOUR TEAM

"Resilience is not about how you endure. It is about how you recharge."
–Sheryl Sandberg, Author of *Lean In*

Resilience in a team is a collective strength.

Resilience is the capacity to quickly bounce back from setbacks, adversity, or tenacity. Failures and setbacks are a given in life, regardless of the perspective you choose, so you must learn to tolerate the sadness and annoyance these mistakes cause. Coping implies that we must support one another in overcoming the challenges, not ignore them.

Building resilience and forming a successful team requires a strong team culture. You can create a successful team by implementing a variety of strategies.

Use the following questions to assess whether your team possesses the traits of a resilient team:

- **How do they deal with one another's candid, open communication and feedback?** To make sure they can recognize and address any issues they may encounter, they must be truthful.

- **When presented with challenges, are they able to generate innovative and practical ideas?** They must possess the resilience to rise to new difficulties. It should be possible for the team to stay concentrated despite external events.

- **Does the group value each other? Do they give a damn about one other's achievements and failures?** Instead of concentrating on their own notoriety or achievements, the most resilient teams work to build up the group.

- **Can they ask each other for assistance?** They must possess the self-assurance to acknowledge the existence of an issue and request assistance. The group uses its struggles to overcome obstacles and come up with answers rather than keeping them a secret.

How do you help your team members develop resilience and cope with challenges effectively?

Resilience is the capacity to handle stress, hardship, and change. It enables team members to overcome obstacles, learn from feedback, and recover from failures, making it critical for team formation.

1. Model resilience.

Setting an example of resilience for others is one of the finest ways to support their development. You can serve as an example by demonstrating how you handle challenging circumstances, manage your emotions, and learn from your errors. You can also talk about how your own experiences with resilience have improved and helped you develop. Offering an example of resilience is one way to encourage people to adopt a similar mindset and attitude.

2. Offer assistance.

Offering assistance to others is another way to help them be resilient. There are several types of support, including practical, emotional, and educational. People can benefit from your listening, empathy, and encouragement when they need emotional assistance. Your feedback, counsel, or resources can be used to provide informational help.

By lending a hand with chores, finding solutions to issues, or delegating responsibility, you provide useful support and make the people around you feel capable, respected, and appreciated.

3. Encourage a growth-oriented mindset.

Possessing a growth mindset means thinking that one can get better at anything by working hard and learning new things. It is essential to resilience because it enables people to accept feedback, perceive possibilities in setbacks, and persevere in the face of difficulty.

By encouraging others to try new things rather than adhere to what they know, by applauding their efforts rather than their results, and by stressing their development rather than their performance, you can help others develop a growth mindset. It is possible to assist people in gaining self-assurance, curiosity, and drive by cultivating a development mindset.

4. Establish a culture of positivity.

A culture that fosters cooperation, trust, and well-being is essential to resilience because it makes individuals feel content, safe, and connected. Having fun and interacting with others, speaking honestly and politely, celebrating accomplishments, learning from mistakes, and creating clear and achievable goals are all ways to foster a great culture within your team. By fostering a good culture, you may encourage people to grow in satisfaction, involvement, and loyalty.

5. Encourage self-care.

Taking care of your physical, mental, and emotional well-being is known as self-care. It is a crucial resilience skill since it helps with stress management, delaying burnout, and energy restoration. Encourage others to take care of themselves by setting an example of good eating, sleeping, and regular exercise, as well as relaxation. By allowing them time, space, and flexibility, you can also show them that you respect their limits. You may support others in achieving equilibrium, resiliency, and well-being by promoting self-care.

Final Thoughts - Chapter 21

Team resilience is a key component of effective performance that many leaders strive for. By incorporating the aforementioned resilience-building ideas, you may better equip your teams to handle obstacles and adjust to changes that may arise in any crisis, both now and in the future.

JOURNAL

How do you help your team members develop resilience and cope with challenges effectively?

_____

_____

_____

_____

_____

_____

_____

_____

_____

_____

_____

_____

_____

_____

22

COACHING AND MENTORING

"I've learned that people will forget what you said, people will forget
what you did, but people will never forget how you made them feel."
–Maya Angelou, Author of *I Know Why the Caged Bird Sings*

One of your main duties as a leader is to support the personal and professional development of the people on your team. You may help people realize their full potential through coaching and mentoring.

Let's examine the value of coaching and mentoring in leadership and talk about practical methods for ensuring the success of your team members while promoting an environment that encourages lifelong learning.

How do you support the professional growth and development of your team through coaching and mentoring?

1. Recognize the distinction between mentoring and coaching.

Coaching and mentoring are complementary yet distinct tools for growth. While mentoring entails sharing knowledge and experiences to direct both personal and professional growth, coaching focuses on improving particular skills and performance.

2. Customize your strategy.

Acknowledge that every team member has distinct goals, shortcomings, and skills. Adjust your mentoring and coaching style to fit each person's requirements and objectives.

3. Establish clear goals.

When mentoring team members, be sure to establish clear goals and expectations. Describe the goals and work together to create plans of action to reach them. When it comes to mentoring, be willing to share advice based on your personal experiences.

4. Give constructive feedback.

A key element of mentoring and coaching is feedback. Provide team members with regular, constructive feedback so they can recognize their accomplishments and pinpoint opportunities for growth.

5. Promote self-reflection.

Team members should be encouraged to reflect on themselves to determine their areas of strength, areas for improvement, and desired careers. Encourage them to explore who they are and assist them in setting reasonable goals for their growth.

6. Establish a safe and supportive environment.

Provide a secure and encouraging setting for discussions. Encourage candid communication and reassure team members that you appreciate their personal development.

7. Provide learning opportunities and resources.

Give your team members tools and educational opportunities to help them improve, such as workshops, training, and access to pertinent information.

8. Lead by example.

Dedicate yourself to your personal advancement, motivating your colleagues to follow suit.

9. Celebrate progress and achievements.

As your team members meet their development objectives, acknowledge their accomplishments and progress. Acknowledgment for their work gives them confidence and inspires them to keep aiming high.

10. Promote peer-to-peer mentoring.

Encourage a culture of mutual support and learning among team members to build a cooperative and empowered workplace.

Final Thoughts - Chapter 22

Coaching and mentoring are useful resources for directing the development of your team members. Adjust your strategy to suit each person's needs and establish precise guidelines for coaching sessions. Encourage self-reflection and offer helpful criticism. Offer tools and educational opportunities to help team members develop their skills and knowledge in a safe and encouraging atmosphere. Celebrate their advancements and success.

By investing in coaching and mentoring, you not only enable your team members to realize their full potential but also cultivate an environment where learning and development never stop. Keep in mind that, as a leader, your dedication to fostering the development of your team members is an investment in both their future and the long-term viability of your company.

JOURNAL

How do you support the professional growth and development of your team through coaching and mentoring?

_____

_____

_____

_____

_____

_____

_____

_____

_____

_____

_____

_____

_____

_____

23

BUILDING TRUST

"The glue that holds all relationships together...
is trust, and trust is based on integrity."
–Brian Tracy, Author of *The 32 Unbreakable Laws of Money and Success*

The currency of leadership is trust. Consider how you nurture and preserve this vital resource with each and every stakeholder in your domain.

Nowadays, there is a lot of talk about trust in the workplace: why it's decreasing, how crucial it is, and how to foster it among your teams. And that makes sense. For many years, leaders' capacity to build trust has been a major factor in determining whether they succeed or fail.

The frequently cited and unattributed adage, "Trust takes years to establish, seconds to shatter, and eternity to restore," still holds true today.

In other words, "It takes 20 years to develop a reputation and five minutes to damage it," as well-known financier Warren Buffet once said. You will act differently if you consider that.

Regarding trust, philosopher Friedrich Nietzsche is credited with saying, "I'm not angry that you told me a falsehood. I'm upset that from now on, I can't believe you."

Having worked with teams and leaders of many different organizations in a variety of sectors, I have witnessed firsthand how trust can help leaders build businesses that exceed their most ambitious goals. I've seen teams and leaders overcome trust challenges and emerge stronger and more capable. I've also witnessed how, without trust, a company may stall out or slow down.

Proper execution leads to strong, trustworthy connections that boost employee engagement, retention, and company outcomes, fostering humanity, empathy, and authenticity.

When employees believe their leaders are "on their side," treat them fairly and with respect, and acknowledge that periodic failures are a normal part of personal development, they feel more trusting in the workplace.

Being trustworthy as a leader involves:

- Keeping your word and acting with dependability and consistency.
- Being personable and amiable (people follow leaders they find trustworthy).
- Promoting compassion, empathy, and sincerity.
- Supporting your teammates through their faults while also owning up to your own.
- Striking a balance between the demand for outcomes and consideration for other people's feelings.
- Putting in a lot of effort to win people over by showing respect for their opinions and viewpoints.
- Making sure your behaviors and words are consistent, not just occasionally but consistently.

Both sides of the trust issue impact a leader's capacity to inspire and encourage staff members. When people trust you, they have faith in your judgment. Your leadership will impact them even in the face of uncertainty. That's because they count on you to follow through on your commitments.

A crucial component of creating trust in the workplace and, eventually, the success of a company is being consistent in both your words and deeds.

Employees frequently report that their impression of a company is mostly shaped by the words and actions of its leaders. Employee engagement and commitment to the company are less likely to occur when there is a mismatch between a leader's words and deeds.

Participation at all levels, beginning with the CEO, is necessary to forge a strong, credible connection that inspires workers to put in the effort required to make their company successful.

Why is workplace trust such a big deal these days?

The fact that trust is seriously declining by many metrics is one of the main reasons leaders need to pay attention to it now.

According to the annual Edelman Trust Barometer, which surveyed 32,000 employees in 28 countries in 2024, trust in businesses with headquarters in the biggest exporting nations—the United States and China—has considerably decreased. Over the previous ten years, American trust in businesses fell by nine points to 53%.

The Edelman poll showed some encouraging trends for the corporate world. Seventy-nine percent of workers said they trusted "my employer." Workers are more inclined to allow their particular leaders greater discretion. However, at 51%, the general level of trust in CEOs is far lower. The public's faith in media and political leaders is also deteriorating.

According to Edelman's research, trust has significantly declined due to the development of artificial intelligence and the fear of an information war. Of all the social anxieties questioned, the fear of an information war (61%) increased by six points from 2023, the largest rise. The survey discovered a rise in the perception that company executives are "willfully attempting to mislead people by expressing things they know are wrong" (61%) among business leaders.

Although employees have higher levels of trust in their own companies, there are indications that this trend is breaking, especially in light of the growing number of hybrid workers and the ongoing trend of workers quitting their employment or reporting high levels of burnout. Based in part on high turnover rates, CEOs stated in a recent study that engaging and keeping staff will be their top priority and problem in 2024.[9]

Without trust in the current economic climate, it is harder to:

- Engage and retain teams and top talent.
- Maintain a strong hybrid or remote workforce culture.
- Create a meaningful employee experience.
- Maintain or build your brand.
- Grow your business and get the results you want.

Given the high rate of employee turnover, leaders have a fantastic opportunity to take advantage of the situation, increase employee trust in the company, and keep their staff.

How do you establish and maintain trust with your team members, stakeholders, and peers?

If you want to succeed as a worker, manager, or leader, you must learn how to establish trust in the workplace. Developing a rapport is frequently the first step towards establishing trust.

It's more challenging to collaborate and communicate with your peers or coworkers if you lack trust. In severe circumstances, a lack of trust may potentially destroy your group or company as a whole. Most people, regrettably, have not been taught how to develop trust.

Stakeholder interactions may go wrong in various ways. Maybe the expectations weren't fulfilled. Alternatively, there may have been a more significant communication failure. But the root cause is generally a basic lack of trust, no matter how large or tiny the reason.

---

[9] https://chiefexecutive.net/new-ceo-survey-finds-retaining-and-engaging-employees-remains-top-priority-and-challenge-for-2024/

Trust is a fundamental component of any relationship when it comes to stakeholder involvement. You should always consider methods to increase and solidify the trust that your stakeholders have in you, even in instances where your stakeholder relationship is fruitful. You never know when a rival may be lurking in the shadows.

How to Build Trust in the Workplace

The following are crucial strategies for fostering trust in the workplace that leaders of all levels can use:

1. Prepare to work for it.

It's been said before that "talk is cheap." You have to win someone's trust, which results from making a deliberate effort to live up to your words, honor your commitments, and conduct yourself in a way that is consistent with your goals and core values. Employees today are sending a message to all levels of firm leadership: if they want to gain trust, they had better put in more effort.

When workers genuinely trust their leaders, they will do everything for them and show more commitment to the company. That implies that one of the most crucial things a leader can do is work on developing trust.

2. Act with integrity and openness.

Tell the truth, not simply what you believe other people want to hear, even if it's uncomfortable. Recognize the information that staff members require and communicate it to them while valuing their work, being sensitive to their emotions, and accepting that mistakes will inevitably occur.

Transparency has been repeatedly noted as being essential to fostering respectful interactions, cooperative efforts, and honest dialogue. It can lessen some of the mystery and suspicion that permeate the workplace and fuel rumors that frequently breed mistrust and doubt.

Consistent and frequent communication should be a top focus to stop rumors from spreading and foster a trustworthy feeling of transparency among staff. Information should be delivered in a timely manner, be pertinent, and be centered on what staff members need to know and why. That being said, transparency does not imply that one must always know the answers. The leaders who are most deserving of trust are not afraid to admit when they are wrong.

A simple way to think about communication transparency is "3 + 1:"

1. "Here's what we know."
2. "Here's what we don't know."
3. "Here's what we're working on finding out."

+1. Aggressively dispel misconceptions. Say, "I want to address something I heard that's not accurate," for instance, and then be specific about what you know and don't know.

3. Listen more intently and deliberately.

One of the biggest errors leaders make is their propensity for overtalking because they believe they must always be in command and steer the conversation.

The truth is that the more time you spend listening, the more critical knowledge you'll gain. This will also advance the company and foster team trust. Workers yearn for a boss who listens to them and values their opinions.

Allowing for silence goes hand in hand with improving your listening skills since such times always lead to greater discourse. While silence is sometimes seen as a void that must be filled, leaders who can embrace it and make use of it give others the chance to voice their opinions and be heard. This not only leads to an increase in knowledge but frequently an unexpected and illuminating relationship as well.

The following are some more crucial techniques for improving listening skills that can help you become a more reliable and trustworthy communicator.

- Provide employees with more avenues to express their issues and queries.
- Resist the need to consider what you are going to say next when a team member is speaking.
- Pay attentive attention to the speaker; avoid multitasking.
- Make sure you understand what's been said by asking questions.
- Summarize what you've heard.
- Keep an open mind, and don't only listen for what you want to hear.
- Observe the things that are not being said.
- Try not to engage in "talking at" your staff; instead, engage in genuine, two-way dialogue.

4. Always demonstrate trustworthy conduct.

Consistently following through on your commitments builds trust over time. Your team must witness your adherence to your personal and team-wide commitments.

Additionally, make a daily effort to listen to your employees and concentrate on improving your connections with them. It is important for the leader's integrity to be evident in how they do business on a daily basis, not simply during quarterly meetings.

For example, if you believe that teamwork is essential to the organization and you personally demonstrate this belief by frequently working as a leader across teams and departments. Give recognition for outstanding teamwork and foster a culture of appreciation and a team-first mindset.

5. Adopt accountability procedures.

Employees see you as credible and will follow your example when you own up to your failures as well as your accomplishments. By implementing procedures that become ingrained in the culture, such as evaluating each project (positives, negatives, things to improve) or including a status report and next actions in the agenda of every meeting (monitoring deadlines and milestones), you can promote responsibility and honest communication.

This strategy also lets team members recognize that you understand that mistakes will be made, but you want to encourage learning from them. It also promotes a culture of continual learning. By doing this, you may increase employee trust since they won't be as afraid to make errors, which is crucial for both innovation and trust.

6. Show your staff compassion and empathy.

Leaders who take a moment to consider their staff members' true feelings and strive to develop sincere connections increase trust. Employees should know that you understand and respect their sentiments. An employee who knows you value them will be the reward, and you'll also have knowledge that will help to inspire that worker.

The following advice will help you interact and demonstrate empathy with colleagues more effectively.

Schedule frequent check-ins for one-on-one or small-group meetings. You and the team/employee may decide upon the frequency, but making sure they happen more frequently shows that you genuinely care and want to have frequent conversations. Give workers time on the calendar to discuss everything, from how they're doing overall to what support or assistance they require from you or management, not just reports on business outcomes.

Find out what your staff is enthusiastic about and keep that in mind. What were their plans for Saturday? To go to a museum, perhaps? To a musical performance? A concert? Do they play golf? Are they fans of any particular sports team? These organic talks strengthen the personal relationship, which inevitably leads to the development of trust.

Express gratitude and provide precise compliments on a regular basis. Highlight the behaviors that you find admirable and impressive to show staff members that you are aware of the excellent job they are doing.

7. Request input and act upon recommendations.

Everyone has been in this situation: After taking the time to submit an employee engagement survey, the employee never receives the findings or sees any leadership adjustments. Leaders must avoid falling into this trap by actively listening and acting upon what they hear. After polling the organization, tell employees what you've learned and what you aim to change.

Once you've asked your team members, "What's on your mind?" or "What might we be doing better?" explain any potential actions you can take and inform staff members of developments. Even if it's not always feasible to reply right away, try to do so after the input has been collected. When you do, be sure to express gratitude for their ideas and help staff understand why you are acting in a particular way or why you might not be able to adopt their strategy or make the change right now.

8. Integrate employee recognition into the organization's culture.

It is important to acknowledge the team. Saying "thank you" for a job well done or taking the time to nominate staff members for your company's recognition program are small but meaningful gestures that have a big impact. In particular, encourage the habits you wish to see persist.

Furthermore, remember that recognition for remote workers might be particularly scarce—but it shouldn't be. For an employee who doesn't often engage with their management or coworkers, the simple things matter a lot. Whenever possible, go above and beyond to acknowledge staff members who meet your needs or answer promptly, even if you aren't face-to-face with them. Emphasize the accomplishments of employees who are difficult to reach throughout team meetings, corporate communications, and virtual offices.

Ways to Build Trust with Stakeholders

It will take time to establish trust with your stakeholder groups. Even successful ventures require patience, commitment, and work to build such trust. Having said that, here are some tactics you may employ to begin building a more robust stakeholder connection.

1. Establish the foundation for a cooperative partnership.

As soon as you meet your stakeholders, you can begin establishing trust by demonstrating your concern for their issues and your desire to learn more about them. How do you go about doing that? Arrange a meeting for discovery.

Meetings for discovery are opportunities to discuss the project or underlying problem and coordinate main objectives. They enable you to define a strategy and project timeframe, remove any doubt regarding the project's scope, and identify any possible risks or challenges. Above all, though, they're a chance for you to demonstrate that you are being truthful and open about the process right from the start.

2. Recognize stakeholders' expectations and requirements.

During your discovery session, it's critical to clarify stakeholders' expectations for you and your project team. Be clear about roles and needs. Ensure that all individuals know their roles, the definition of success, and the process for providing feedback. At this point, you should show that you are proactive and consider how you will continue to establish and uphold trust for the duration of the relationship.

3. Have reasonable expectations for yourself.

As they say, trust is a two-way street. Thus, when establishing expectations, be careful to consider what you might reasonably expect from your customer.

Even though it would be ideal for you to receive feedback on your deliverables on the same day, it might not be feasible. There may be too many project stakeholders, or they are working on several projects concurrently. Instead, collaborate with them to set expectations that complement your objectives and theirs. Consideration like this demonstrates empathy, a necessary component of trust.

4. Develop a plan for engaging stakeholders.

Creating a plan that explains which stakeholders you should involve in each phase of your project and their preferred mode of interaction and communication will not only help you stay organized and productive but will also demonstrate that you are putting their needs first and adhering to their preferred procedures for getting approval and getting in touch with them for important decisions. It's also a fantastic method to increase trust and fortify positive bonds in partnerships.

Stakeholder mapping is an efficient way to develop your engagement strategy. Consider it a reference guide for identifying and comprehending the relationships among your primary stakeholders. If you employ any of the several methods available, such as a network diagram or grid system (a tool used to visually review and analyze relationships and influence), it will be simpler to operate and communicate with your different stakeholders in their preferred manner.

5. Use warm-ups to establish common ground.

Encouraging comfort and engagement among stakeholders is another aspect of building trust. This is sometimes difficult, particularly at the beginning when you're still getting to know one another and discovering your working methods. For this reason, using warm-ups might be a good way to step outside of your comfort zone and break down some boundaries.

Warm-ups are an opportunity to relax, have fun, and use creativity to help everyone feel comfortable. Anything goes as long as it's enjoyable and promotes interpersonal understanding. You may, for instance, go around the room and ask everyone to share a memory of a previous residence. Alternatively, you may ask everyone to tell a tale about their very first job. There are countless options.

You may warm up online with a variety of methods, even if your team is remote or hybrid. Try some out to discover how they enhance teamwork and foster enduring bonds with others.

6. Adopt a radical transparency policy.

It's simple to see why radical openness is a good idea—after all, who doesn't like being informed and up-to-date, particularly when it comes to complicated projects? But it can be harder to develop radical transparency as a habit.

Establishing a regular time to provide updates and project progress on a weekly or monthly basis, depending on the project timetable, is a smart place to start. You may even set up a shared board to regularly publish updates for interested parties to view and respond to, mentioning important benchmarks and performance indicators even if they fall short of projections.

You should also maintain a record of every meeting note, paying particular attention to action items and possible problems. In addition to keeping your stakeholders informed, you should aim to anticipate any challenges before they become significant. Because of this sort of responsibility and forethought, openness breeds trust.

7. Be steady and dependable.

Consistency is essential to building stakeholder trust since it makes planning and work easier. Stakeholders should be aware of when updates will be sent and if deliverables will be delivered on schedule. They should also be made aware that they will receive the assistance they require when needed.

Perhaps more significantly, though, is that being dependable conveys your concern for and appreciation of their time. They won't have to speculate as to when they will hear from you or whether they will receive all that they require. By performing your job properly, you're simplifying their task.

8. Provide chances for regular follow-up and feedback.

Making it as simple as possible for your stakeholders to communicate, provide feedback, and follow up can ease the process of offering criticism—which is sometimes seen as the most challenging part of working partnerships.

Make an effort to provide as many opportunities as you can for your stakeholders to share their ideas and opinions. This may be as simple as setting out five minutes for free-flowing conversation at the conclusion of each meeting. Alternatively, it can include proactively contacting them on a frequent basis to inquire about their thoughts on your advancement. This shows that you value their opinion and want them to participate, which is a fundamental element of a trustworthy relationship.

9. Approach disagreement as a chance to address problems.

Conflict will inevitably arise at some point. Your team may be unable to agree on a certain project aspect or a particular stakeholder may be challenging to collaborate with. Despite your best efforts, disagreement is inevitable, but by fostering trust, you can be prepared to handle it when it arises.

Strive to see every disagreement as a chance to figure out a solution. First, acknowledge the issue right away and then have a candid discussion to find out exactly what's wrong. If you can identify areas of agreement, such as a shared project aim or value, you may start the process of working toward a settlement. When looking for answers, use your imagination and exercise patience. Your reward will be stakeholders who are even more confident in your expertise.

10. Recognize when to confront stakeholders.

While it's crucial to pay attention to your stakeholders, including their ideal working style, desired outcomes, and definition of success, another necessary skill is being able to fight back against their beliefs and expectations while still coming off as knowledgeable and trustworthy.

This can be challenging, but when executed properly, it can be highly productive. Clearly identifying the subjects in which your staff is knowledgeable should be the first step. As a design expert, for example, you don't have to accept every design suggestion from your stakeholders. Instead, take the risk of challenging them when you believe there's another way you can add greater value. They will probably value your honesty if you are keeping in mind their bigger objectives and expectations.

Final Thoughts - Chapter 23

Gaining the trust of stakeholders is a gradual process. You should establish your commitment to this procedure from your first conversations with them. Demonstrate that you truly care about their continuing needs, are committed to openness, and intend to communicate honestly and frequently. Regularly putting these techniques into practice may require time and work on your side, but the payoff will be a more fulfilling and fruitful connection for you and your stakeholders.

JOURNAL

How do you establish and maintain trust with your team members, stakeholders, and peers?

_____

_____

_____

_____

_____

_____

_____

_____

_____

_____

_____

_____

_____

24

ACCOUNTABILITY

"Accountability breeds response-ability."
–Stephen R. Covey, Author of *The 7 Habits of Highly Effective People*

Accountability ensures the integrity of action, contributing to a positive and encouraging work environment. Professionals should strive to accept personal accountability, hold one another responsible, and promote an accountability-based company culture as a whole, as all of these contribute to a more effective work environment.

When everyone in a company accepts responsibility for their actions, there is accountability. Employees at all levels, from recent hires to senior executives, should have this expectation.

There are several ways in which professionals might demonstrate accountability at work. Anyone can embrace personal accountability if they acknowledge their duties and resolve to carry out their assigned roles within the organization. This may entail fulfilling certain obligations or criteria.

A few instances of individual responsibility in the workplace are as follows:

- Attending work for the agreed-upon hours
- Independently completing all responsibilities included in the job description

- Completing all other assigned tasks
- Maintaining a satisfactory and consistent quality of work
- Collaborating with peers and accepting the division of labor
- Communicating with management about updates or challenges

Accountability for leaders in the organization extends to their team's performance. Leaders who invite everyone to submit their performance data and goals can foster a climate of accountability.

Greater responsibility may be possible for the organization as a whole. This might involve senior management setting clear expectations for the company's values, mission, and goals and requiring all workers to meet the same equitable standards. It may also mean accepting responsibility for the company's deeds and results, both deliberate and accidental, locally and worldwide.

How do you hold yourself and others accountable for their actions and performance?

Being responsible to others and yourself is one of the most crucial parts of being a leader. Being responsible means accepting accountability for your deeds, keeping your word, and making sure others follow suit. Building trust, encouraging teamwork, and attaining organizational success all depend on accountability.

Holding oneself and other people accountable, though, is not always simple and calls for perseverance and dedication. Let's look at some successful leadership strategies that will enable you to hold yourself and others accountable. These useful tactics are applicable in personal and professional contexts, and it doesn't matter how big or complicated your company is.

We'll discuss the significance of establishing unambiguous expectations, giving regular feedback, and setting a positive example. We'll also go over how to respond to difficult circumstances, such as missed deadlines or subpar work, with professionalism and empathy.

Accepting these fundamental accountability concepts can help you become a more successful leader who motivates people to perform to the best of their abilities.

1. Establish clear expectations and successfully communicate them.

Efficiently defining and conveying expectations is a crucial component of holding oneself and others responsible. It is your duty as a leader to make sure that everyone on your team is aware of what is expected of them and what will happen if those expectations are not reached. This means establishing precise objectives, laying out due dates, and specifying the range of duties.

It is crucial to communicate these expectations to your team clearly and consistently. This promotes a sense of ownership and accountability among team members and prevents confusion and misunderstandings. Establishing trust and responsibility via excellent communication and clear expectations will make your team more successful and productive.

2. Establish repercussions for failing to live up to expectations.

Setting clear expectations for yourself and the people you oversee is essential for leaders. But simply establishing expectations is insufficient. Setting up repercussions for failing to live up to such standards is also crucial. Positive or negative consequences are both possible, but they must be appropriate to the offense.

When workers know there are repercussions for not living up to standards, it encourages them to prioritize their jobs and take responsibility for their actions. Enforcing sanctions consistently is crucial for leaders to prevent any perceptions of partiality or unjust treatment. Effective leadership requires keeping oneself and others responsible. Establishing clear penalties for failure to meet standards can also assist in creating an environment of accountability.

3. Consistently enforce consequences.

Consistently enforcing consequences is one of the core ideas of holding oneself and others accountable. Establishing clear consequences for both positive and bad performance, defining roles and duties, consistently enforcing penalties, and setting norms and expectations are all necessary to create an accountable culture.

Leaders need to be prepared to confront subordinates who don't perform up to par, offer helpful criticism, and hold staff members accountable for their work. When leaders' authority is undermined by their repeated failure to enforce sanctions, it can lead to a culture of entitlement where bad behavior is accepted. Strong leaders who regularly enforce punishments create an environment of responsibility that encourages positive conduct, pushes staff to put in more effort, and eventually results in the accomplishment of company objectives.

4. Encourage candid dialogue and constructive criticism.

A culture of accountability, in which individuals are held accountable for their actions and results, is necessary for effective leadership. To create this kind of culture, candid criticism, and communication are essential. Leaders should provide a friendly, comfortable environment where team members may express their thoughts, worries, and suggestions and offer helpful criticism.

Leaders are better equipped to see areas for development and progress and to comprehend the challenges that their team is facing. Fostering a culture of open communication and feedback increases team members' sense of accountability and ownership, increasing their level of investment in the group's and the company's overall success. Furthermore, it fosters an atmosphere of openness and trust between parties, both of which are necessary for developing solid and fruitful professional ties.

Leaders who place a high priority on open communication and feedback make their team members feel heard, respected, and empowered to contribute to the success of the organization.

5. Lead by example and accept responsibility for your actions.

Establishing an accountable culture within your team or business is crucial for you as a leader. Setting a good example and being responsible for your actions are two of the finest methods to do this. This means accepting responsibility for your errors, being forthright and honest about them, and making the required amends. Team members are inspired to follow their leader's example when they witness them accepting accountability for their conduct.

As a leader, you should clearly define success for your team or organization and set clear objectives and goals. It should be a top priority to periodically check in with your team members to make sure they are progressing as planned and to offer resources and help when required. By setting a good example and taking responsibility for your actions, you can create an accountability culture that inspires your team or organization to attain its maximum potential.

Final Thoughts - Chapter 24

In conclusion, effective leadership requires the ability to hold oneself and others accountable. Leaders may exercise accountability by establishing clear expectations, offering feedback, being open and honest with their team, and modeling the desired conduct. Holding people accountable can be difficult, but it's essential for the team's long-term success. These pointers can help leaders establish an accountable culture that fosters development, productivity, and a happy workplace.

JOURNAL

How do you hold yourself and others accountable for your and their actions and performance?

_____

_____

_____

_____

_____

_____

_____

_____

_____

_____

_____

_____

_____

25

CONFLICT RESOLUTION

*"Peace is not absence of conflict; it is the ability
to handle conflict by peaceful means."*
–Ronald Reagan, 40th President of the United States

C onflict, when managed well, can be a gateway to innovation. Resolution techniques are necessary since human interaction can occasionally result in conflict. Negotiation, or conflict resolution, is a means by which the parties in conflict can work out a compromise that will satisfy everyone.

Conflicts can be resolved by a neutral third party, mediator, or engaged party who examines the situation from a different angle to find a solution.

Resolving disputes amicably is frequently regarded as a leadership quality. Organizations highly value individuals who can recognize problems, accept differing viewpoints, and foster consensus. These individuals increase the likelihood that people will put aside their differences to get the job done.

How do you navigate conflicts within your team and facilitate productive resolutions?

Managers who employ this strategy are likely to be able to diffuse conflict before it gets out of control.

1. Be proactive.

Whether it's due to excluding someone from an email exchange, saying something improper, or talking over others in a meeting, conflict frequently begins with little arguments that quickly get out of hand.

Therefore, if you see a conflict, take action rather than passing it off to human resources or your teammates to handle. This demonstrates your serious approach to conflict and refusal to support possibly harmful behavior.

2. Observe.

Although indications of conflict might be subtle, you can detect them by observing how members of your team communicate with one another. People's tone of speech, facial expressions, and body language may all reveal conflict.

The more familiar you are with your teammates, the easier it will be to read indications and identify any hidden conflicts. Remember that you might also need to consider whether conflicting values are causing the tension in addition to the specifics of the dispute.

3. Act impartially and fairly.

Make sure you maintain your objectivity even if you agree with one or more team members who are in conflict. It is your responsibility to address the problem that is causing the conflict and come up with a solution that benefits both sides.

4. Be fair to everyone.

Allow everyone the space and time to express their opinions and address any criticism. All sides must be able to present their case and get equal attention.

THE POWER PLAY JOURNAL

5. Intervene when required.

Don't let anybody overpower more reserved coworkers or take over the conversation. If someone is continuously talking over other people, focus your queries on the offending individual.

If the person continues to try to interrupt, please ask them to wait until their colleague has completed before presenting their own viewpoint.

6. Steer clear of assumptions.

When resolving conflict, avoid asserting things that you merely believe to be true or that you have heard. It's advisable to use expressions like "As far as I'm aware" or "As I understand it," for instance.

This indicates that you are aware that what you think might be incorrect, and it offers the disputing parties a chance to reiterate their positions and clear up any misconceptions.

7. Listen actively.

Paying close attention to what the other person is saying is the main goal of active listening. Salespeople frequently employ this ability to establish a stronger connection with clients during a presentation, but it's also a universal quality that every true professional should be able to do.

The most crucial thing you can do to engage in active listening is to keep your ears and mind open. In addition, pay attention to figuring out the other person's objectives, and don't hesitate to clarify things when you're unclear about them.

Try paying attention to how the other person expresses things while handling conflict. After that, reply in exactly the same terms. This helps dispel any misunderstandings regarding the topics being covered and shows that you paid attention.

Final Thoughts - Chapter 25

Resolving conflicts is an art and a very important one at that. It is not just a duty. The way we handle conflict as leaders affects the direction that our teams and organizations take. We not only resolve problems but also promote a collaborative and innovative culture by addressing them with empathy, clear communication, and a solutions-oriented mentality. Recall that constructive conflicts are essential to development.

Accept conflict as a tool for personal development. Launch a candid conversation among your group members and see how constructive conflict can have a transformational effect.

JOURNAL

How do you navigate conflicts within your team and facilitate productive resolutions?

_____

_____

_____

_____

_____

_____

_____

_____

_____

_____

_____

_____

26

FEEDBACK AND RECOGNITION

"We all need people who will give us feedback.
That's how we improve."
–Bill Gates, Co-Founder and Former CEO of Microsoft

Feedback is the breakfast of champions.
Providing feedback may be quite tense. Indeed, it causes people's hearts to race. Although it's not an easy task, it's a crucial aspect of your work.

Feedback may help achieve effective teams and better employee performance. The objective is to give constructive rather than destructive feedback, whether you're conducting performance evaluations or need to address a specific difficulty.

Constructive feedback concentrates on the activities and behaviors that a person might adopt to advance in life. Although it may be difficult for team members to take in constructive feedback at first, it ultimately provides them with direction for growth and makes them stronger.

Destructive feedback, on the other hand, undermines people and saps their self-esteem, which can impair staff morale. It depresses people about themselves and their work.

Fortunately, if you take the proper precautions, you can prevent this. Positive feedback, which includes compliments, encouragement, and acknowledgment of accomplishments, is crucial for boosting team spirit and promoting output.

Naturally, things don't always work out. It may sometimes be essential to call a worker's attention to an error or, more broadly, to less-than-optimal work habits. When presented negatively, this is criticism, which may be upsetting for your coworkers to hear and can feel extremely personal.

By providing constructive feedback, you may find solutions and make positive progress, all while highlighting problems in a way that may not feel as harsh or personal to your team members. This can be a highly successful strategy for handling challenges and optimizing team performance.

How do you provide constructive feedback and recognize the achievements of your team members?

Feedback is one of the most important ways to communicate at work.

Giving feedback is essential for the learning and development of your team and informing your staff of how they are doing and what is expected of them. This feedback must be provided consistently throughout the year, not just at performance assessments.

How can a manager or team leader provide constructive feedback to staff members?

Suggestions for providing constructive feedback are listed below.

1. Be specific and problem-focused.

Not only should you point out areas for improvement to an employee, but you should also explain why you are doing so. Saying to an employee, "You need to be arriving to work sooner," for instance, presumes that they understand the significance of timeliness. Instead, define the real issue at hand and center your feedback on it.

The employee may lack complete background information or context. Give them an idea of how the problem impacts you and the rest of the company. Your feedback will be more actionable the more detailed you can be with it.

2. Discuss the circumstances, not the person.

Positive feedback is, by its very nature, objective and results-oriented; it does not consider the employee's personal qualities. Individual-focused feedback may be interpreted as an assault driven more by sentiment than objective truths.

By talking about the situation, you're demonstrating that you're more interested in finding a solution than in berating the worker.

3. When praise is deserved, give it.

It's important to give positive feedback to staff, and highlighting achievements in the midst of setbacks will help convince them that you're still in control. For example, you might say, "Sales are up 13% over the previous quarter. I think you did a fantastic job with this account. However, a few clients have informed us that response times have gotten longer." This lets the worker know that while you're not dissatisfied with their work in general, you are pointing out key areas that need improvement. Take caution not to oversell the advantages since this might come across as untrue.

4. Be straightforward but not formal.

Avoid sending feedback by text or email to prevent misunderstandings and make what you're saying appear less significant. The ideal way to communicate is to find a private area where you can have an open and sincere conversation with the employee one-on-one. If that isn't feasible or if you normally communicate via phone or video chat, those options can also be effective.

Even if you want to seem casual, it's better to get right to the point because any kind of feedback works best when it's concise.

5. Be truthful.

If your tone and demeanor don't align with the content of the feedback, you risk sending your employee a confusing message.

If the feedback is favorable, let your feelings show that you value their efforts. Addressing unfavorable feedback with a stern tone will demonstrate that you think the issue needs to be treated seriously. (Never deliver unfavorable feedback when you are upset because what you say can have an unintended consequence with your HR department!) Above all, always strive to keep your negative emotions—like sarcasm, rage, or disappointment—to yourself.

6. Pay attention.

Make sure your employee has an opportunity to react to the problem or issue before you give them constructive feedback. You two should have a chat about it. This demonstrates that you're willing to hear their concerns and their version of what happened. Additionally, it's an opportunity for the staff member to share ideas with you and contribute to the solution.

7. Make it timely.

It's ideal to commend a worker when their accomplishment is still new. For negative feedback, timeliness is equally crucial unless the employee has done something that truly hurts your feelings. If that's the case, it might be best to discuss it with them after you've "cooled off." This may ensure that your feedback remains impartial and uninfluenced by feelings. (The worst thing you could do as a leader is wait for a performance review to communicate negative feedback. Everyone deserves an opportunity to course-correct and grow from these experiences. Not delivering negative feedback in a timely manner is a disservice to the individual and the other staff to whom you will eventually delegate the work. Additionally, it is not an effective use of your time if you end up doing the work yourself.)

Final Thoughts - Chapter 26

The finest form of constructive feedback exudes support and respect and concentrates on behaviors or circumstances rather than individuals. Good constructive feedback encourages workers to reach their full potential by helping them identify and avoid errors.

Remember that everyone benefits from praise, so don't expect staff members to always be aware of their good work; instead, acknowledge it with them. Giving employees regular feedback, whether it's good or negative, is one of the most crucial and effective employee development strategies you can employ.

JOURNAL

How do you provide constructive feedback and recognize the achievements of your team members?

_____

_____

_____

_____

_____

_____

_____

_____

_____

_____

_____

_____

_____

27

INNOVATION AND CREATIVITY

"Innovation distinguishes between a leader and a follower."
–Steve Jobs, Co-Founder and Former CEO of Apple

Innovation is the fuel for success. Maintaining a culture that values creativity and innovation is essential for staying ahead of the curve in the fast-paced corporate landscape. Having a fantastic product or service is not enough; your company has to constantly innovate and foster innovation. This means establishing an environment at work where taking calculated risks is not only accepted but appreciated and where each team member feels empowered to participate in the company's creative process.

How do you encourage a culture of innovation and creativity within your team to drive continuous improvement?

Creativity and innovation are not merely catchphrases in the busy hallways of contemporary business; they are essential to the success of businesses. Remaining competitive and relevant requires the capacity to cultivate an atmosphere where ideas bloom and novel solutions take root.

1. Accept failure.

If your company is to genuinely foster innovation and creativity, it must accept failure as a necessary step on the path to success. Remind your team that not every concept will succeed and that they should take measured risks. By eliminating the negative connotation associated with failure, you create an atmosphere where workers are more inclined to put forth audacious, unconventional ideas without worrying about the consequences. This willingness to try new things is essential to innovation and can produce ground-breaking results.

2. Diverse teams.

Innovation is powered by diversity. Bringing together teams with a variety of ages, genders, ethnicities, cultures, and professional experiences creates a melting pot of viewpoints that may inspire original solutions to challenging issues. Promote cooperation and ensure that every voice is respected and heard. The synergy of varied ideas leads to a more creative and inclusive culture, which is necessary for innovation to flourish.

3. Continuous learning.

To foster innovation, an environment of ongoing learning is essential. Give your team the chance to learn more and develop their skills with online courses, workshops, and seminars. Employees who are knowledgeable about the newest developments in technology and trends might contribute original ideas. A dedication to education also communicates your appreciation for the professional growth of your team, which can inspire innovation and raise spirits.

4. Honest communication.

A creative organization's foundation is its open lines of communication. Promote communication among all staff members, from interns to executives. People are more willing to contribute creative ideas when they believe that their opinions are valued and taken into consideration. Frequent brainstorming meetings and public discussion boards can help foster this kind of dialogue, making sure that creativity is a shared endeavor rather than the exclusive purview of a small number of people.

5. Reward creativity.

Maintaining a creative culture requires valuing and rewarding creativity. Recognizing innovative efforts via incentives, possibilities for professional progress, or public recognition inspires others to think creatively. Make sure your incentives program is in line with your innovation objectives so staff members realize their innovative efforts matter and are essential to the company's success.

6. Adaptable setting.

A flexible work atmosphere greatly fosters creativity. Encouraging workers to work from home, set their own schedules, and design their own workplaces can boost morale and productivity. People are frequently more creative and productive when they work with methods that best suit their unique requirements and interests. A flexible approach shows that you trust your team to properly manage their personal time while being dedicated to the company's creative goals.

7. Feedback and iteration.

Similar to how a conscientious gardener takes care of their plants, organizations also need to provide feedback and iterate on their creative endeavors. Establish strong channels for gathering input, such as an open-door policy, frequent surveys, or special feedback sessions, to help you improve your creativity and innovation projects and make sure they keep growing and changing.

Final Thoughts - Chapter 27

In the larger picture of organizational success, creativity, and innovation are the threads that turn aspirations into realities. Organizations can unleash the limitless potential of their teams and create a garden of limitless possibilities by cultivating a psychologically safe environment, embracing diversity, offering rich environments for creative exploration, accepting failure as a growth-promoting catalyst, encouraging cross-pollination through collaboration, harvesting the fruits of creative labor, and tending to the garden with feedback and iteration.

JOURNAL

How do you encourage a culture of innovation and creativity within your team to drive continuous improvement?

_____

_____

_____

_____

_____

_____

_____

_____

_____

_____

_____

_____

_____

28

TIME MANAGEMENT

"The key is in not spending time, but in investing it."
–Stephen R. Covey, Author of *The 7 Habits of Highly Effective People*

Time is a leader's most precious resource. You must invest a lot of time and effort into being a leader. However, even the most committed leaders may experience burnout if they don't successfully control their energy levels. It's critical to understand that your well-being affects your capacity to lead.

This chapter will walk you through the necessary measures to ensure you're properly recharging so you can keep motivating and leading your team without running out of steam.

How do you prioritize tasks, manage your time effectively, and avoid burnout as a leader?

1. Prioritize tasks.

The first step in effective time management is to rank things according to their urgency and significance. Being a leader means that you frequently have a ton of things to handle. You may direct your energy where it is most required by determining which chores need to be completed right away and which can wait. This not only makes it easier to manage your workload but also ensures that you aren't wasting your energy on unimportant tasks.

2. Establish boundaries.

Keeping your energy levels stable requires setting clear boundaries. This entails allocating certain times for work and relaxation, ensuring that neither overlaps with the other. Being available all the time may seem necessary to a leader, but it may quickly cause burnout. As crucial to the success of your team as your active leadership is, make sure you have time to refuel by communicating your availability to them and keeping to it.

3. Delegate effectively.

One essential leadership trait that might help you maintain your energy is delegation. Entrust jobs to team members who possess the necessary skills. Giving your team ownership over their job empowers them, and it also frees up your time and mind so you can concentrate on advanced strategic planning and thinking. Keep in mind that the goal of delegation is developing a solid team capable of sharing the burden—it does not mean giving up control.

4. Control stress.

Stress is an aspect of leadership that cannot be avoided, but it can be managed. Create stress-reduction strategies that you find effective, such as exercise, meditation, or engaging in hobbies that divert your attention from your work. By including these activities in your daily routine, you may keep your mind clear and composed. This will help you make wise judgments and maintain the endurance needed for successful leadership.

5. Recharge regularly.

Taking frequent breaks throughout the day can help you better manage your energy. Frequent short breaks from work-related tasks might also help you avoid mental exhaustion and sustain high production levels. To keep your mind active and focused, think about using strategies like the Pomodoro technique,[10] which involves working for a predetermined amount of time and then taking a quick break.

6. Daily reflection.

At the end of each day, evaluate how effectively you controlled your energy levels. Examine your performance history, your overall mood for the day, and your areas for improvement. This regular practice helps you identify trends that deplete your energy so you can modify your routine as needed.

Final Thoughts - Chapter 28

In mastering time management, the key lies in harmonizing priorities, boundaries, delegation, stress control, and daily reflection. By prioritizing tasks effectively, setting clear boundaries, delegating wisely, managing stress, and making time for regular self-reflection, leaders can maintain their productivity without succumbing to burnout. Embrace these strategies to not only enhance your efficiency but also to sustain your well-being and lead with resilience and clarity. The path to effective leadership is paved with mindful time management and the commitment to balance your professional and personal life.

---

[10] https://todoist.com/productivity-methods/pomodoro-technique

JOURNAL

How do you prioritize tasks, manage your time effectively, and avoid burnout as a leader?

29

CONTINUOUS LEARNING

"We now accept the fact that learning is a lifelong process of keeping abreast of change. And the most pressing task is to teach people how to learn."
–Peter F. Drucker, Author of *The Effective Executive*

The landscape of knowledge is ever-expanding. The most successful people tend to learn something new nearly every day, and the most prosperous companies also do this. Cultivating a continuous learning culture is critical for an organization. It is the cornerstone of organizational development and the catalyst for creativity and flexibility.

How do you prioritize your professional development and encourage a culture of continuous learning?

Building a culture of continuous learning is essential for a business. It is the cornerstone of organizational development and the creative force behind adaptation and innovation.

These are some of the most crucial actions you should take to create a continuous learning culture inside your company.

Start by getting top leadership to commit to making continuous learning a priority. I want to be really clear about this: A culture of continuous learning did not exist, does not exist now, and will never exist if you are a training and education leader without the full support of your senior leadership. When leaders stress the value of learning, it sets the tone for the whole organization.

Explain the advantages and importance of continuous learning to everyone in clear detail. Teach them that learning encompasses more than simply personal development. It also has to do with enhancing output. The goal is to improve job happiness. It's about being competitive in a rapidly changing world.

Motivate your staff to establish personal learning objectives. The objectives should align with the organization's and their own professional growth. These objectives may be linked to certain competencies, knowledge bases, or skill sets. They ought to be pertinent to their current responsibilities or future roles they aspire to take on.

Make sure each team member has several learning resources available. Programs for internal training, seminars, online classes, mentorship, and coaching may fall under this category. Consider providing a varied selection of possibilities to accommodate a diversity of learning preferences and styles.

Urge the people under your supervision to arrange consistent time for learning in their work schedules. This could take the shape of set "learning hours" or adaptable work schedules. These need to enable people to engage in learning activities without impeding their productivity.

Establish an atmosphere that promotes exploration, experimentation, and information exchange. Encourage people to ask questions, get feedback, and share what they've learned with others. Recognize and reward people who participate actively in learning activities.

Encourage a culture where errors and setbacks are viewed as chances to learn rather than as reasons to assign blame or administer punishments. Promote risk-taking, experience-based learning, and knowledge-sharing.

Team members should receive regular feedback on their progress in learning. Provide constant direction in areas that need improvement. Encourage open communication regarding learning and growth amongst team members and management.

Organize group projects and team-based learning exercises to promote cooperation and cross-functional learning. Provide a learning atmosphere where staff members may benefit from each other's knowledge and experience.

Senior leaders should be curious about the efficacy of educational initiatives. They should create measurements and assessment techniques to monitor the results of programs for continuous learning. They should also evaluate the training programs' efficacy. Participant input should be gathered, and learning opportunities should be improved and refined using data.

Organizations that learn more often have higher earnings. Regarding people, the same is true. In the dictionary, "earn" comes before "learn," but in real life, the reverse is true. Before you can *earn*, you must first *learn*.

Final Thoughts - Chapter 29

Building a culture of learning is a continuous endeavor. It calls for perseverance, support, and flexibility in response to shifting circumstances. One way to foster an atmosphere that supports development, innovation, and continuous improvement in a business is to promote a learning mentality among all employees.

JOURNAL

How do you prioritize your professional development and encourage a culture of continuous learning within your team?

30

PERSONAL GROWTH AND DEVELOPMENT

"Become a student of change. It is the only thing that will remain constant."
–Anthony D'Angelo, Editor of *75 Years of Impact and Influence*

Leadership is a personal evolution.

Effective leadership is a continuous learning and development journey, not a destination. Prioritizing personal development helps leaders better negotiate the challenges of their jobs, motivate their teams, and propel organizations toward success.

Changes in technology, social values, organizational dynamics, and the corporate environment all affect how leadership changes over time. Proficient leaders understand that to tackle these changing obstacles, they need to change and develop. Here are some reasons why leaders need to engage in continuous learning and development:

Enhanced Problem-Solving

Every day, leaders must make several difficult decisions and solve a variety of complicated problems. Constant learning increases their knowledge base and gives them a variety of tools and perspectives to successfully address these problems.

Adaptability to Change

In today's rapidly changing environment, leaders need to be flexible and receptive to new concepts and methods.

Making critical decisions that may have long-term effects is a common responsibility of leadership. Leaders have the knowledge and abilities to make wise, well-informed decisions via continuous learning.

Improved Communication Skills

Effective leaders rely greatly on communication. By engaging in continuous learning, leaders may enhance their communication abilities, such as active listening, empathy, and the ability to communicate their ideas and vision.

Enhanced Emotional Intelligence

Successful leadership requires a high degree of emotional intelligence, which includes social skills, self-awareness, self-regulation, and empathy.

Talent Development

Developing talent within a company is another duty of successful leaders and serves as the backbone of organizational success.

Enhanced Leadership Styles

There is no one-size-fits-all approach to leadership. Various circumstances could call for various leadership styles. By building a flexible toolset of leadership skills, leaders may adjust their style to suit different situations and team dynamics. This is also made possible via ongoing learning.

How do you prioritize your personal growth and development as a leader to continue learning and evolving?

Consider the following strategies to promote continuous learning and individual growth as a leader:

1. Establish specific learning objectives.

Determine the areas in which you wish to advance as a leader. These goals are related to leadership abilities, business acumen, and individual development.

2. Make a learning plan.

Describe how you want to accomplish your learning goals. This strategy might be going to workshops, enrolling in classes, reading books, looking for a mentor, or engaging in online forums for your industry.

3. Encourage a growth mindset.

Having a growth mindset means that you think that intellect and skill can be acquired with commitment and hard work. A willingness to learn from mistakes and losses is a hallmark of this mindset.

4. Stay informed.

Read, go to conferences, and network with colleagues to stay up to date on industry trends, new technology, and best practices.

5. Seek mentorship.

Guidance and insights from seasoned leaders can be obtained through mentoring. Mentors may guide you through your leadership path, provide guidance, and share their experiences.

Find leaders you respect and appreciate, and learn from their accomplishments and leadership strategies.

Final Thoughts - Chapter 30

Develop an inquisitive mindset by remaining inquiring. Make inquiries, investigate novel concepts, and maintain an open mind to other viewpoints.

There is no separation between leadership and personal growth. Influential leaders are dedicated to continuous development and learning because they recognize that leadership is a never-ending journey.

JOURNAL

How do you prioritize your own personal growth and development as a leader to continue learning and evolving?

_____

_____

_____

_____

_____

_____

_____

_____

_____

_____

_____

_____

_____

_____

31

SUCCESSION PLANNING

"Leaders who don't listen will eventually be surrounded by
people who have nothing to say."
–Andy Stanley, Author of *Better Decisions, Fewer Regrets*

The future is built today. Succession planning is an essential procedure that any firm should perform to guarantee continuity, stability, and a strong corporate culture. This means locating and nurturing future leaders inside the company to guarantee a seamless leadership handoff in the event that present leaders retire, step down, or die.

Succession planning is crucial for an organization's long-term viability. It guarantees that a company has a pool of qualified and experienced leaders ready to step in and take over when existing leaders depart. Thanks to succession planning, organizations can provide training and development opportunities for their staff to address those gaps. It also helps identify possible shortages in leadership skills and knowledge.

Additionally, succession planning fosters a culture in which workers are appreciated, feel important, and are given various levels of authority. Employee engagement and commitment are higher when they perceive possibilities for growth and progress. This can, therefore, raise production levels, boost staff retention rates, and improve the organization's overall success.

How do you identify and develop future leaders within your organization to ensure a smooth transition of leadership roles?

The Importance of Succession Planning

It's not only about filling vacancies when it comes to succession planning. Such planning is a calculated move to protect an organization's future by making sure it has a group of capable people who can take on leadership positions with ease. The following benefits justify the need for succession planning:

- **Transfer of Knowledge:** When skilled workers retire or leave, they take a plethora of institutional knowledge with them. Succession planning preserves the organization's wisdom and best practices by passing this information on to the next generation of leaders.

- **Talent Development:** Putting money into the training of upcoming leaders produces a workforce that is both competent and driven. Recruiting and keeping top personnel promotes a culture of continuous learning and progress.

- **Business Continuity:** If a company does not have a suitable succession strategy, it may experience instability and disturbances during leadership changes. Succession planning helps to reduce these interruptions and ensures that operations continue uninterrupted even in the event of key staff's departure.

- **Risk Mitigation:** Any firm can face difficulties due to external reasons like recessions or sudden employee departures. By creating a pipeline of future leaders prepared to take over, succession planning reduces these risks.

Crucial Components of Succession Planning

For a business to create a successful succession planning program, three essential components must be taken into account:

- **Determine Critical Positions:** First, determine the important roles in your company. These might be technical specialists, leadership roles, or jobs in charge of important tasks or initiatives. Evaluate your present staff to find people with the drive and talent to fill these critical positions in the future. This examination might include performance reviews, skill reviews, and evaluations of leadership potential.

- **Plans for Development:** After possible successors have been identified, prepare for their development. Training, mentoring, and exposure to assignments and projects with higher visibility that prepare them for the duties of the desired jobs are all a part of this. Encourage seasoned employees to teach prospective successors and impart their knowledge. This promotes a seamless transfer of duties and helps bridge the generational divide.

- **Review and Feedback:** Make necessary adjustments to your succession plan on a regular basis. To ensure the strategy stays applicable and successful, solicit feedback from both present leaders and possible successors.

Putting Succession Planning into Practice

The following actions should be taken when putting succession planning into practice within your company:

- **Take the Lead:** Time is of the essence for successful succession planning. Start the process far ahead of anticipated changes in leadership to enable adequate time for planning and development.

- **Involve the Parties:** Involve important stakeholders, such as HR advisors, senior leaders, and possible successors, in the planning and execution process. Their opinions and experiences are insightful.

- **Communicate Openly:** Employees should be made aware of your company's succession planning initiatives. This can inspire courage in people to take an active interest in their own development and foster a positive, aspirational environment.

- **Employ Technology:** A variety of instruments and software solutions are available to assist with succession planning, making it simpler to locate and monitor possible successors and their development progress.

- **Track Development:** Monitor prospective successors' advancement on a regular basis and evaluate how well your succession strategy is working. As organizational demands change, adjustments and improvements should be made as needed.

Final Thoughts - Chapter 31

In today's corporate climate, succession planning is essential, not optional. Businesses that put succession planning first and execute it well will be better equipped to handle the upheaval of changing leadership, hold onto their competitive advantage, and guarantee long-term success. Organizations may secure their continuous growth and prosperity by developing a pipeline of leaders capable of guiding the ship into the future through the identification of critical positions, talent assessment, and development initiatives. Planning for tomorrow should begin right now.

JOURNAL

How do you identify and develop future leaders within your organization to ensure a smooth transition of leadership roles?

_____

_____

_____

_____

_____

_____

_____

_____

_____

_____

_____

_____

_____

_____

32

BUILDING A LEGACY

"Carve your name on hearts, not tombstones. A legacy is etched into the minds of others and the stories they share about you."
–Shannon L. Alder, Inspirational Author and Therapist

E very leader leaves a legacy. How do you want your leadership to be remembered? If someone were asked about your leadership, what would they say about you? The narratives that others tell about you reveal a great deal about your character and abilities as a leader.

A lot of people put off considering their leadership legacy until the very end of their professional lives. Instead, it ought to be your primary emphasis when you first start your profession. What impression do you wish to leave on others? What kind of leader do you want to be, and are you making an effort to be that kind of leader every day?

Scott Mabry is a leadership coach and writer known for his focus on emotional intelligence, personal growth, and organizational culture. As I read his article "The Leader's Imprint,"[11] it occurred to me how big an "imprint" a leader's every decision and deed may have on those under them. In the 2016 article, Mabry argues that an imprint remains on the staff following the

---

[11] https://susanmbarber.com/category/confidence/page/5/

activities and strategies employed by a leader in response to a crisis situation. Regularly being critical of our teammates affects them in the long term. Individuals depart from managers rather than organizations. When someone is overly critical, they start to question themselves, shut down, lose interest in the work, or quit.

What matters most is how you respond to people and events. They may overcome failure by adopting a positive mindset, asking constructive questions, offering support throughout setbacks, and advocating for them in public. Without worrying that they will lose your favor or receive criticism, they may try new things, take risks, and grow more resilient.

This is similar to a parent who is unrelentingly critical of their child. The child starts to question their talents and self-worth and believes that their parent no longer loves them. The imprint left behind by this parent is the childhood trauma of emotional abandonment.) While workers learn from their leaders, children learn from their parents. Be the leader that the rest of the group looks up to.

Without First Making Time for You and Your Needs, You Can't Leave a Great Leadership Legacy

You have a daily plan that, depending on your circumstances, can consist of meetings, conference calls, doctor visits, kid activities, supper, grocery shopping, etc. This has the feeling of being an endless merry-go-round. When will you have time to sit down and consider your options? Because so many other people are vying for your time, you most likely don't.

How do you envision your life unfolding? What kind of legacy would you like to leave? These are really important considerations that could seem overwhelming, but you must give them some thought. If not, you might regret it later in life, and by then, it might be too late.

I've come to the realization over the last few years that my actions and goals were slightly out of alignment. When I was riding the merry-go-round every day, I was unaware of it. I was packing more and more useless activities into days that were already overextended.

Looking back, I'm not really sure how I managed to accomplish it all as I was also navigating health challenges. It truly freed me up to prioritize, be more creative and explore new opportunities as soon as I left that pressure cooker environment. I decided to be selective and focus on what I wanted to do; what I wanted to contribute; and what I wanted to offer.

What if, for a few hours over the weekend, you began to reflect on your true desires? Just start asking yourself the question; you don't have to have all the answers at once. It's not easy stuff, and a lot of my customers ask themselves the same questions when they come to me.

Observe the daily events going on around you. Which actions do you wish you were taking? What are the plans you've had for years but never got around to executing? Which tasks do you consistently put off till you have more time? The lesson here is to start listening to those things and then figure out how to implement them. This means that you should find a way to prioritize your tasks over the ones that other people want you to perform. Make the conscious decision to allocate your time and attention to the areas you desire.

Your Legacy Will Be Memorable

Recall the reasons behind your selection as a leader. As a leader, it is your duty to establish the group's direction, organize the group to accomplish its goals, lead by example, and cultivate the next generation of leaders. Consider the influential leaders in your professional life and the ways in which they facilitated your progress. Choose the legacy you wish to leave behind for your team and your organization.

What kind of legacy do you want to leave behind as a leader, and how are you actively working toward building that legacy within your organization and beyond?

It's normal for a leader to think about the legacy they have left behind. People's memories of you are a reflection of your influence, your morals, and how you have shaped those around you. It's crucial to think about your legacy as a leader and the kind of impact you want to have, whether you're leading a group, an organization, or even a community.

1. Lead by example.

Leading by example is one of the best ways to leave a lasting impression as a leader. Since words don't always translate into deeds, when you act with integrity, honesty, and accountability on a regular basis, you encourage others to follow suit. Establishing the tone for your team and making a lasting impact requires exhibiting a strong work ethic, empathy, and dedication to personal growth.

2. Foster a positive and inclusive culture.

A leader who cultivates a welcoming and upbeat culture will be well-remembered. Creating an environment where everyone feels valued, respected, and included fosters a sense of belonging and courage. In addition to improving your team's overall performance, diversity and acceptance of other viewpoints help you leave a legacy of harmony and equity.

3. Encourage and develop others.

A leader who makes an investment in their team members' growth and development will be seen as a mentor and a force for success in both personal and professional spheres. Through facilitating learning opportunities, providing constructive feedback, and enabling others to take on novel challenges, you foster self-confidence and facilitate the realization of individuals' full potential. Long after you are gone, the influence of what you have done for other people will endure.

4. Have an impact on other people's lives.

Leaders who impact other people's lives are frequently the most admired and remembered. Demonstrating empathy and compassion, whether by generosity, mentoring, or just being there for people when they need you, creates a lasting impression. You can leave a legacy that goes long beyond your time as a leader by going above and beyond the call of duty in your line of work and showing real concern for the welfare of those around you.

5. Encourage adaptability and innovation.

Leaders who encourage innovation and flexibility will be hailed as pioneers in today's quickly changing world. To make an impression as a forward-thinking leader, promote a creative culture, adopt new technology, and challenge the existing status quo. By creating an environment that welcomes change and supports experimentation, you enable people to push boundaries and have a lasting influence.

6. Express yourself clearly and openly.

A key component of excellent leadership is effective communication. Build trust and encourage open channels of communication among your team by speaking with clarity, transparency, and sincerity. A leader who conveys a clear vision, gives timely feedback, and actively listens will ensure that people understand what they're saying. This degree of communication guarantees that your leadership style will be positively remembered, in addition to improving teamwork.

7. Leave a legacy of continuous learning.

A leader who emphasizes continuous learning and fosters a growth mindset creates a legacy of inquisitiveness and progress. By emphasizing personal development and cultivating a culture of learning within your team, you can encourage people to adopt new information and abilities. In addition to helping people, this dedication to continual learning fosters a culture of innovation and flexibility that will last long after you have left.

Final Thoughts - Chapter 32

It takes more than accomplishments and awards to be recognized as a leader. It is all about the long-term effects you have on the culture you cultivate and the people you lead. By leading by example, encouraging diversity, enabling others, learning a difference, pushing innovation, communicating clearly, and placing a high priority on continuous learning, you will leave a legacy that will be remembered long after you are gone. So, give some thought to the kind of leader you want to be and the kind of legacy you want to create.

JOURNAL

What kind of legacy do you want to leave behind as a leader, and how are you actively working toward building that legacy within your organization and beyond?

FINAL THOUGHTS
THE LEADERSHIP JOURNEY

As the final pages of this journal brim with the ink of your reflections, know that the end of this book is not the conclusion of your journey. Leadership is an odyssey without a destination—a path of perpetual growth, learning, and transformation.

My hope is that *The Power Play Journal* has served as your map through the rich terrain of leadership principles, challenging you to introspect, adapt, and aspire to greater heights.

Your journey through these pages has been unique, marked by your insights, challenges, and triumphs. Perhaps some questions sparked a light of recognition, while others stirred a storm of contemplation. This is the essence of authentic leadership—the courage to question, the strength to grow, and the wisdom to evolve.

As your life and career progress beyond this journal, carry with you the profound understanding that leadership is a force that moves, shapes, and inspires. It is the subtle art of balancing vision with action, empowerment with accountability, and innovation with tradition.

Reflect upon the moments of epiphany, the strategies developed, and the plans laid down. Consider this journal not merely as a repository of past thoughts but as a springboard into the future. Your musings and meditations are the seeds of future endeavors, the foundation upon which you will build tomorrow's triumphs.

Remember my journey—from the spirited streets of Southeast DC to the esteemed halls of leadership. Let it remind you that your origins do not define you; your choices do. Leadership is not bestowed. It is cultivated with each decision, each relationship, and each challenge faced with courage and integrity.

My accolades and acknowledgments are not merely laurels to rest upon but beacons that light the path for those who follow. As you continue to lead, think of the legacy you wish to create. How will the lessons learned here be reflected in the lives you touch and the institutions you shape?

Leadership is an echo that resonates through the halls of time long after our voices have fallen silent. It is the values instilled in a team, the inspiration drawn from a vision, and the change enacted through persistent, passionate endeavors.

In closing, do not view this as the final chapter but rather as a momentary pause to gather your strengths before continuing the ascent. The summit of leadership is ever-rising, and with each step, you are called to reach higher, delve deeper, and lead with greater purpose.

Carry forth the spirit of inquiry and the flame of inspiration that *The Power Play Journal* has ignited within you. Share it generously, wield it wisely, and may it light your way as you forge ahead on the unending adventure of leadership.

Through my example and these pages, I've tried to impart a message of resilience, transformation, and relentless pursuit of excellence. May your leadership journey be as impactful and fulfilling as the path she has carved, and may your story inspire the leaders of tomorrow just as I have tried to inspire you today.

ACKNOWLEDGMENTS

This book was challenging to write for many reasons. Over the years, I have been reflecting and taking notes, implementing strategies that could work, might work, didn't work, and some that were incredibly effective. The big lesson I learned is that these strategies mean absolutely nothing if you do not care about the people you work with and for and who support you. If you think otherwise, you are missing the mark.

Leadership is not about being the boss. Leadership is not about having a title. Leadership is not about telling people what to do. Leadership is about trust, influence, and inspiration to motivate, act, and execute. Without trust, you have no influence. Without influence, you cannot inspire anyone or motivate them to act and execute anything to fruition. If no one is listening to you, this is why. If no one is getting anything done, this is why. If you don't have the respect of your team, this is why.

Leadership is quite simple. Let's stop overthinking this. Think back to when you started your career and what you needed from your boss or leader. Be the person you needed back then because that is the same person we all need now. We need leaders who care to listen. We need leaders who recognize when something's not right and step in to fix it. We need leaders who understand that some expectations of staff are just not fair, feasible, or appropriate, and sometimes, they're downright wrong.

When you become the leader who has the trust, influence, and inspiration to motivate, act, and execute, anything that you ask of your team will get done. Trust me. I have seen it time and again.

I want to acknowledge all the people who inspired me through their leadership and influence, starting with my parents, Ernest S. Davis and Josefina Jamito Davis. My father served in the U.S. Marine Corps for 20 years, managing and supporting the family from abroad, while my mother worked a full-time job in hotel housekeeping and raised five children simultaneously. I lost both parents when I was in my 20s, but reflecting on their hard work, tenacity, and resilience has inspired the principles by which I live my life and work with purpose.

I am so thankful to my maternal grandmother, Candida Aguilar, who always cared for me and created an environment of safety and warmth, and to my husband and best friend, Maurice Jackson, the most supportive, disciplined, consistent, protective, and loving person I have ever known. I am grateful for the over 30 years we've been together and look forward to many, many more.

To my godmother, Christine Drayton, who dedicated her career to the U.S. Senate—you have been a tremendous inspiration to me as I've navigated my own life and career. Your unwavering support for me and my family, even before I was born, has been a constant source of strength.

To Scott Bensing, my first chief of staff in the U.S. Senate, who cared enough to boldly pull me aside and call me out on my attitude. That candid conversation meant the world to me, as it was the first time someone told me the truth about how I was being perceived professionally. It led me to embrace significant management responsibilities and became a major catalyst for my work in emotional intelligence.

To Sharon Fountain of Performance Development Consultants, LLC and my success coach, over the last 15 years, your coaching has helped me navigate environments with pretentious attitudes, superiority complexes, dominating personalities, and individuals with an overinflated sense of self-importance.

With your support, my resolve has significantly strengthened; my leadership acumen has become highly developed and refined; my confidence is now calm, steady, and powerful. Your noteworthy precedent has inspired me to share my value with others, create meaningful change, and influence outcomes for as many leaders as possible.

To Richard Walters, for recognizing and harnessing my value through opportunities that allowed me to showcase my strengths in meaningful ways. I appreciate your friendship and support.

In reflecting on the opportunities and experiences that have shaped my journey, I recognize their incredible impact. Though some moments were stressful and unfavorable, I know they were molding me into the leader I am today—one who can adeptly navigate organizations, develop and leverage talent, and help others achieve success through innovative organizational management frameworks, power-dynamics coaching, and self-mastery. My life's purpose is to create successful outcomes through self-awareness, motivation, and transformation, and to stand with others on their journey toward greatness.

As you embark on your journey, remember this: "The greatest leaders are not those who have never faced adversity, but those who have turned challenges into stepping stones and transformed vision into reality. Harness your power, lead with purpose, and inspire greatness in others."

CONNECT WITH ME

*T*he *Power Play Journal* is just the beginning. For those who seek to dig deeper into the art of leadership and harness their full potential, an invaluable opportunity awaits. If the insights you've uncovered here resonate with you and you're ready to elevate your leadership to an even higher level, consider the transformative experience of working directly with me.

By scheduling a strategy session with me, you can learn more about my program offerings, which are tailored to executives and emerging leaders alike. These sessions provide a personalized touch to your leadership journey, offering various engagements with a seasoned expert who has walked the path and navigated the terrain of high-stakes leadership environments.

My coaching philosophy is anchored in real-world experience and a deep understanding of the dynamics that drive successful leaders and organizations. My bespoke coaching and mentorship programs are crafted to meet you where you are and propel you to where you want to be. Whether you're looking to refine your strategic thinking, enhance your emotional intelligence, or innovate within your leadership style, my guidance unlocks your potential and catalyzes your growth.

To learn more and to schedule your strategy session, contact me directly by scanning the QR code at the end of this book. Embrace this chance to invest in yourself and your leadership legacy. Join me and take a definitive step toward crafting your future in leadership with clarity, confidence, and strategic power.

Remember, the leadership journey is continuous, and the path to excellence is best navigated with a trusted guide. Let me be that guide for you.

ABOUT THE AUTHOR

Tinna Jackson is a native Washingtonian and student of leadership, and this journal encapsulates the wisdom gleaned from over 28 years of experience across an array of sectors. Tinna is not just an executive and power dynamics coach but a celebrated conduit for change whose expertise in emotional intelligence and strategic operations has been the cornerstone of a remarkable career.

Tinna's leadership narrative is a testament to her multifaceted expertise, from the intricate corridors of national politics to the dynamic spheres of nonprofits and trade associations. As a strategic operations and personnel management architect, former deputy chief of staff in the U.S. Senate, and distinguished C-level executive, she has deftly navigated the complex mazes of power and policy.

At the heart of Tinna's success lies her intrinsic capacity to forge authentic connections, rallying a mosaic of talent to pivotal roles that resonate with purpose and potential. Her transformative impact is mirrored in the operational transformations she has engineered, the innovative environments she has cultivated, and the strategic partnerships she has fostered.

Through Jackson Consulting Group, LLC, Tinna channels her vibrant communication style, collaborative spirit, and rich experience to steer organizations and leaders toward the pinnacle of their potential. Her dedication to empowering the vanguard of executive leadership is recognized and revered, and she has received accolades that acknowledge her prowess and passion, such as being named Empowered Woman of the Year and the Top Executive Coach of 2024 by the International Association of Top Professionals.

THANK YOU FOR READING MY BOOK!

Just to say thanks for buying and reading The Power Play Journal, I would like to give you a complimentary strategy session with me!

Scan the QR Code:

I appreciate your interest in my book and value your feedback as it helps me improve future versions of this book. I would appreciate it if you could leave your invaluable review on Amazon.com with your feedback. Thank you!

Made in the USA
Middletown, DE
19 September 2024

61158000R00142